John Newton, famo[...]
that "none but He who[...]
pel." Indeed, faithful p[...]
of the church. Brian Cr[...]
a thoughtful, theologically engaged practitioner; and a source of sound
wisdom on matters of ministry.

Dr. Albert Mohler, president of The Southern Baptist
Theological Seminary

Brian Croft gives advice on shepherding that is biblical, illuminated
by the wisdom of godly pastors of the past, and eminently practical.
Here is a system for praying for every member of the church, suggestions
on how to encourage widows, encouragement to faithfully uphold the
doctrines of Holy Scripture, and more—all in one book! I highly commend it to both seminary students and seasoned pastors.

Dr. Joel R. Beeke, president of Puritan Reformed Theological
Seminary in Grand Rapids, Michigan

What a helpful book! Ten clear pastoral priorities, each one biblically
grounded and practically expounded. This book will be a huge blessing to many shepherds and even more sheep. I wish it had been around
when I was starting out in ministry twenty years ago.

David Murray, professor of practical theology at Puritan Reformed
Theological Seminary and author of *How Sermons Work*

The key to a successful pastoral ministry is not how gifted a man is
but how he sets his priorities and keeps to them, despite pressures all
around. And the best priorities are those that follow biblical rather than
pragmatic demands. Here Brian Croft goes to the Scriptures and identifies the God-given priorities that will give any pastor ballast to keep him
stable on the long and narrow stretch for many years.

Conrad Mbewe, pastor of Kabwata Baptist Church
in Lusaka, Zambia

I highly recommend the how-to nature and tone of *The Pastor's Ministry* to steward the office of pastor well. God has instructed us how we
are to live and lead as shepherds, and we would do well to heed Brian
Croft's wisdom in implementing these truths. I pray that God will use
this book to encourage and disciple a new generation of godly shepherds.

Daniel Montgomery, lead pastor and founder of Sojourn
Community Church, Louisville, Kentucky, and author of
*Faithmapping* and *Proof*

With a pastor's heart, Brian Croft succinctly summarizes the work of pastoral ministry, offering wise counsel for both the aspiring and the practicing pastor. Few authors speak with such clear, practical advice about the daily workings of pastoral ministry. Because he is a pastor himself, Brian gets the mechanics of ministry and offers helpful insights for maintaining a healthy ministry. Brian's advice about scheduling prayer is in itself worth the price of the book.

> Dr. Greg Cochran, associate professor and director of the applied
> theology program at California Baptist University

My friend Brian Croft shares here the very principles and practices of pastoral ministry that are so often neglected and quickly forgotten. Whether you need instruction or correction, learning or reminding, Brian's gift for simple and clear communication of plain pastoral realities will clear your head, warm your heart, and strengthen your hands.

> Jeremy Walker, copastor of Maidenbower Baptist Church
> in Crawley, England, and author of *A Portrait of Paul*

Whenever pastors approach me with questions about pastoral ministry, I refer them to Brian Croft's materials. Instead of combing through reams of helpful information on his website, the reader is offered a "one-stop shop" resource in *The Pastor's Ministry*. Croft offers scripturally rich, gospel-saturated, practical shepherding advice for the minister of congregations of any size. This won't be a book you file away on the shelf, but one you will reference throughout your ministry.

> Robby Gallaty III, PhD, senior pastor of Brainerd Baptist Church
> in Chattanooga, Tennessee, and author of *Growing Up*

Brian Croft is a wise pastor whose writings have significantly shaped my own understanding of pastoral ministry. Reading *The Pastor's Ministry* has been encouraging, convicting, challenging, and refreshing. As an elder, I heartily commend this book to my fellow pastors, whether you are just starting out in gospel ministry or are a seasoned shepherd of God's flock. As a seminary professor, I recommend it to every student who "aspires to be an overseer" (1 Timothy 3:1).

> Dr. Nathan A. Finn, elder at First Baptist Church of Durham,
> North Carolina, and associate professor of historical theology and
> Baptist studies at Southeastern Baptist Theological Seminary

# the
# pastor'sministry

QG 03-21-17

# the pastor'sministry

## BIBLICAL PRIORITIES FOR FAITHFUL SHEPHERDS

## Brian Croft

ZONDERVAN

*The Pastor's Ministry*
Copyright © 2015 by Brian Croft

This title is also available as a Zondervan ebook. Visit www.zondervan.com/ebooks.

Requests for information should be addressed to:
Zondervan, 3900 Sparks Dr. SE, Grand Rapids, Michigan 49546

ISBN 978-0-310-51659-0

All Scripture quotations, unless otherwise indicated, are taken from The Holy Bible, *New International Version®, NIV®.* Copyright © 1973, 1978, 1984, 2011 by Biblica, Inc.® Used by permission. All rights reserved worldwide.

Scripture quotations marked NASB are taken from the *New American Standard Bible.* Copyright © 1960, 1962, 1963, 1968, 1971, 1972, 1973, 1975, 1977, 1995 by The Lockman Foundation. Used by permission.

Any Internet addresses (websites, blogs, etc.) and telephone numbers in this book are offered as a resource. They are not intended in any way to be or imply an endorsement by Zondervan, nor does Zondervan vouch for the content of these sites and numbers for the life of this book.

All rights reserved. No part of this publication may be reproduced, stored in a retrieval system, or transmitted in any form or by any means—electronic, mechanical, photocopy, recording, or any other—except for brief quotations in printed reviews, without the prior permission of the publisher.

Cover design: Christopher Tobias/tobiasdesign.com
Interior design: Kait Lamphere

Printed in the United States of America

15 16 17 18 19 20 /QG/ 19 18 17 16 15 14 13 12 11 10 9 8 7 6 5 4 3 2 1

To Mark Dever and in memory of Jackson Boyett—
the two men who most deeply shaped
my understanding of pastoral ministry;
I owe a great debt to you both.

# Contents

# Contents

# Foreword

Have you heard the old story about the reluctant Civil War soldier? He couldn't decide which side to fight for. So he went into battle wearing the dark blue pants of the Union army and the gray coat of the Confederates. Of course, when the confused young man showed up for battle, shots came at him from both directions.

Unfortunately, this is the reality many of us face as Christian pastors. We suffer from an identity crisis. Yes, we are called pastors, but what does that really mean? Without a doubt, the word of God gives a clear explanation of a pastor's call and work. And throughout church history, the biblical role and responsibilities of a pastor have been clear. We are to be shepherds who lead and feed our flocks to spiritual maturity and fruitfulness in Christ. Christian pastors are to lead the congregation to be faithful in doctrine, holy in lifestyle, and united in fellowship. Our goal is Christ-centered, Scripture-based, gospel-driven congregations where the glory of God is put on display before the watching world.

But many contemporary pastors have lost sight of what we are called by God to be and do. We are soldiers who do not know which side we are fighting for.

Many pastors base their ministry on business models. These models have led many pastors and churches to focus on pleasing customers and attracting prospects. The goal is "church growth." It is a sad indictment that for many pastors the term *church growth* is associated with numbers, statistics, and resources rather than with the spiritual development of those saints the Lord has placed under our spiritual care.

As a result, many pastors today spend their time in ministry trying to meet the felt needs of their members. Some of these pastors compromise by trading the standard equipment of Christian ministry for bells and whistles that will attract more people. This is inevitably frustrating, because these felt needs constantly change at the whim of human opinion, interest, and experience.

It is a vicious cycle because the more we focus on the felt needs of our members, the more they will expect the same medicine for their self-diagnosed ailments. And the more we focus on putting on a show to attract the world, the more people will expect the lights to be brighter, the stage to be bigger, and the production to be glitzier. The pastor who fails to keep up with the demand can become a victim of spiritual burnout. And the one who succeeds is in even greater spiritual danger.

But there is a more excellent way. It is God's way—the pastoral ministry taught in the New Testament. It is ministry that keeps the main thing the main thing. It is a call to be a shepherd and not a rancher, an overseer and not a manager, a pastor and not a celebrity. It involves dedication to prayer and the ministry of the word. It is a committed focus on the tasks of preaching the word, leading in worship, visiting the sick, counseling the troubled, and comforting the bereaved. It is living an exemplary life. It is … well, it's about being a pastor.

In *The Pastor's Ministry*, Brian Croft calls pastors back to the basics. Brian has a heart for the gospel, the church, and the glory of God. And he loves pastors. I have benefited from his mentorship from afar through the resources found on his *Practical Shepherding* blog and through the books he has written. I heartily commend this clear, biblical, and practical explanation of the work of the pastor to every man of God who desires to hear the Master say, "Well done, good and faithful servant."

H. B. Charles Jr., pastor of Shiloh Metropolitan Baptist Church, Jacksonville, Florida, October 2014

# Introduction

> Be shepherds of God's flock that is under your care,
> watching over them ... And when the Chief Shepherd
> appears, you will receive the crown of glory that will
> never fade away. **1 Peter 5:2, 4**

Everyone is busy. This is the reality of our modern culture. There is work that needs to be done, a family to care for, a house and car to maintain, friendships to cultivate, doctors to visit. There are kids' activities to schedule and guests to host. For those of us who are Christians, we can add to the normal busyness of life our attendance at church and possibly volunteering in one of its ministries (or for another organization) once a week. Life in the twenty-first century feels like an unending rat race. We only slow down when crisis and sickness force us to take a break.

Those who pastor God's people experience many of the same pulls, pressures, demands, and responsibilities as other Christians. And because a pastor is called to be involved in the lives of the people in his congregation, he must learn to juggle his own schedule with the hectic schedules of his church members as well. Their busy lives create additional tension in ministry, setting many pastors up for failure—even before they begin.

Many pastors fall into two traps here. In some cases, a pastor quickly realizes he cannot provide adequate care for his congregation, so he doesn't. Even with a smaller congregation, it's not possible to pay a hospital visit after *every* surgery, attend every ball game, officiate every funeral, sit in on every committee meeting, accept every invitation to come over for dinner, participate in every church workday, and respond to every counseling request. Discouraged, some stop trying altogether. A pastor may choose to focus more broadly on administrating large activities, managing busy programs, and overseeing the general functioning of the local church, leaving the "work of ministry" to others—or neglecting it altogether.

On the other hand, some determined pastors recognize they can't do it all, but they commit to pushing through the pain. They put an ambitious hand to the plow and hope that with enough effort they will at least please *some* people. This approach has its own dangers, though. The pastor is now enslaved to the demands and needs of his church. The congregation, whether directly or indirectly, largely determines how his time is spent. His ministry faithfulness and fruitfulness will be based on how happy his congregation is with his efforts, and while some will be pleased, there will always be people who are never satisfied. Satisfying people becomes his way of measuring faithfulness, yet it will leave him feeling exhausted and empty.

## The Pastor's True Biblical Calling

A pastor is not called to run programs for the masses, nor is he called to do it all and try to please everyone. God is the one who calls pastors to ministry, and the specifics of that calling are clearly outlined in God's word. The only way a pastor can avoid these pitfalls and remain steadfast throughout his life and ministry is to know *what* God has truly called him to do—and to do it! The apostle Peter exhorts elders/pastors to be shepherds[1]—to care for God's people:

> Be shepherds of God's flock that is under your care,
> watching over them—not because you must, but
> because you are willing, as God wants you to be; not
> pursuing dishonest gain, but eager to serve; not lording

it over those entrusted to you, but being examples to
the flock. And when the Chief Shepherd appears, you
will receive the crown of glory that will never fade away.

**1 Peter 5:2–4**

Peter's exhortation to pastors can be summarized in a single
sentence: "Be shepherds of God's flock under your care until the
Chief Shepherd appears." And in case you missed it, Peter is pretty
clear about the who, what, when, and how of a pastor's biblical
calling.

- **What:** "Be shepherds of God's flock."
- **Who:** The "flock that is under your care."
- **How:** "Not because you must, but because you are willing,
  as God wants you to be; not pursuing dishonest gain, but
  eager to serve; not lording it over those entrusted to you,
  but being examples to the flock."
- **When:** Until "the Chief Shepherd [Jesus Christ]
  appears" — returning for his flock placed in your care.

A pastor's true calling, then, is to shepherd the souls of God's
people humbly, willingly, and eagerly, and to do all of this on
behalf of the Chief Shepherd, Jesus Christ. This has not changed
from the time Peter wrote these words until today. Though our
culture has changed and life is radically different today than it
was in the first century, the basic responsibilities of pastoral ministry have not changed.

The word of God is sufficient to provide us with an outline of
a pastor's divine calling and to instruct in how he should prioritize
his daily schedule. God's word consistently highlights the priorities of faithful shepherds and affirms that these priorities revolve
around the core calling — to "be shepherds of God's flock that is
under your care." God's word has the power to cut through the
demands, pressures, and expectations that crush a pastor's spirit.

For you pastors, my hope is that by studying and meditating

on the calling and priorities of pastoral ministry you will better understand *what* God is truly asking of you and *where* he wants your time to be spent. The aim of this book is simple: to reveal the priorities that God sets for every pastor. God reveals these priorities throughout Scripture. He establishes them in the life of Israel, roots them in his full redemptive plan, and confirms them in the instructions he gives through Jesus and the apostles. This book will focus on ten key priorities that are at the heart of every pastor's ministry.

*1. Guard the truth.* A pastor must be committed to the word of God and the apostles' teachings and be willing to preach, teach, and defend them when they are contrary to the culture.

*2. Preach the word.* A pastor must faithfully preach the whole counsel of God's word, carefully explaining the meaning of the text and applying it to the lives of those under his care.

*3. Pray for the flock.* A pastor should be an intercessor, bringing the needs of his church before God and modeling prayer both publicly and privately.

*4. Set an example.* A pastor is an example to his flock and should always be aware that others are looking to him as a model. While a pastor should model righteous behavior, he must also model confession and repentance, acknowledging he is also a sinner and teaching his people how to apply the gospel to life.

*5. Visit the sick.* Pastors should visit those who are sick and in need of care and encouragement, and they must train others in the congregation to help care for those in need.

*6. Comfort the grieving.* In the face of death, a pastor should grieve with those who grieve and should sensitively remind those who are grieving of the hope and encouragement of the gospel. This involves preaching gospel-focused messages at funerals and graveside services.

*7. Care for widows.* This much-neglected biblical teaching calls for pastors to be responsible for the widows of the church and to find creative ways to model care for widows by involving their families and other members of the church in caring for these special women.

8. *Confront sin*. Pastors need to confront sin and lead the church in the exercise of discipline in the hope of repentance and restoration.

9. *Encourage the weaker sheep*. Though we can be tempted to easily dismiss people who are slow to change, God calls pastors to model patience and persevering hope by working with those who are difficult, despairing, and challenging.

10. *Identify and train leaders*. It is the primary responsibility of pastors to identify, train, and affirm leaders in the church. Every pastor should have a plan for doing this in his local church and should be actively seeking out the next generation of leaders.

Each of the priorities listed above will be grounded in an exposition of God's word and practically fleshed out in the context of life and ministry. We need to be biblically grounded in these pastoral imperatives before we can develop the practical tools to engage in these tasks.

## An Important Caveat

As you see these ten priorities, you may be curious about the absence of other important aspects of a pastor's ministry, such as evangelism and caring for the poor. Paul exhorts Timothy to do the work of an evangelist (2 Timothy 4:5), and he instructs the churches in Galatia to remember the poor (Galatians 2:10). To be sure, these are important responsibilities that are necessary to the health of any local church. They are also areas in which a pastor should lead, model, and encourage his church. However, in this book I focus on the priorities of a *shepherd's* ministry—the things he must do to care for God's people in particular. Even though I have not directly addressed these important ministries, expect to find some mention of them woven throughout the ten priorities. Evangelism is necessary as we preach the word and guard the truth. Caring for the poor in the church is inevitable as a pastor visits the sick, cares for widows, and encourages the weak.

Ultimately, I want every pastor who feels the burdens and pressures of ministry and who deals with the impossible expectations of shepherding people to experience freedom from the bondage of meeting every need, giving away time that is not available, trying to be in two places at once, and maintaining countless unappreciated, head-spinning tasks. My hope is that the power of God's word expounded in these pages will invigorate every pastor to see what God desires for his life and ministry and to better discern what he can do that will please the Chief Shepherd.

part 1

# foundation

## Chapter 1
# Guard the Truth

> What you heard from me, keep as the pattern of sound
> teaching, with faith and love in Christ Jesus. Guard the
> good deposit that was entrusted to you—guard it
> with the help of the Holy Spirit who lives in us.
>
> **2 Timothy 1:13–14**

Every father feels a protective instinct toward his own children. And sometimes that means he must overcome his own fears to protect them.

I struggle with a strong and healthy fear of large, mean-looking dogs. Sometimes when I run through our neighborhood, I carry a stick with me, just in case I encounter one on a run. At times, I change my route just to avoid attracting the gaze of an unchained canine.

On one particular sunny afternoon, I was walking down the street with my family when a large, angry dog suddenly broke out from a neighbor's front door that had carelessly been left open. The dog zeroed in on our family. He began charging at full speed directly toward my youngest daughter as she rode her bike, and in that moment, I put aside my personal fears. I was consumed by one thing—an innate desire to protect my daughter, no matter the cost. I was ready to do whatever was necessary to make sure she was kept safe.

Thankfully, everything ended well. No one was hurt. And I didn't have to hurt any dogs that day either! The owner came out in the nick of time and whistled for his dog, and two hours later, my adrenaline level returned to normal.

In that moment when I first saw the dog charging at my daughter, I reacted instinctively. Sure, there was a moment of fear, and several thoughts flashed in my head, but I wasn't debating the consequences right then. I knew that only one thing mattered—making sure my daughter was safe.

What does this have to do with being a pastor? As a pastor who also regularly cares for and advises other pastors, I know there are many things a pastor needs to be doing. There are sermons to preach, sick members to visit, burdens of leadership and administration to bear. And yet God has called pastors to a unique role, one they bear not just for their local churches but for the kingdom of God. Pastors are called to be guardians of the truth. And like a father protecting his daughter from attack, this calling requires courageous, sacrificial action. A pastor must care for his people, yes, but it means guarding them and guarding the truth by protecting them from false teaching. It means helping them understand and grow in the good news of God's word.

Why is this the first thing I mention? Because if we lose the truth, we have nothing left to give our people.

God has made his truth known to his people throughout the ages, and in every generation he has called and equipped certain men of God to be the protectors, stewards, and guardians of the truth. Busy pastors trying to minister to busy people in our modern world must learn and embrace this biblical priority, or there will be nothing left to say and no one left to hear it. The doctrines and beliefs of the church, rooted in the Scriptures, are the lifeblood of the church. If we fail to guard the truth, the good deposit of God's word, nothing else will matter.

## Biblical Guardians of Truth

The Bible tells us God chose one nation from all the other nations of the earth to be his people and told them he would be their God. That nation was Israel—a people born of Abraham and his faith in God. God chose to reveal himself and his ways to his people through the words he spoke to them. The same voice with which God spoke and created the universe from nothing would be the means by which God would communicate his perfect character, his sovereign purposes, and his redemptive ways. After Moses led Israel out of bondage in Egypt, God brought them to a place in the wilderness and made a covenant with them. God spoke the terms of the covenant to Moses to share with the people, and the people agreed to God's terms (Exodus 19). God spoke his law to his people, giving them blessings for obedience and curses for their disobedience. And Moses wrote all of this down. These words became the terms of their relationship, the law that would guide Israel's future. Even when the people disobeyed, God continued to make himself and his word known to his people, preserving his word throughout the generations.

In the years of the kings, many of Israel's rulers did great evil in the sight of the Lord, yet God was still moving in the hearts of his people making himself, his promises, and his plan known. He moved the hearts of some in Israel to delight in the law of the Lord and to meditate on it day and night (Psalm 1:2). In each generation, God revealed there was a small remnant of his people who continued to love his law, delighting in its precepts and walking in God's ways (Psalm 119). The prophets carried the torch forward, guarding the law by speaking the truth about what God had revealed. Though they were regularly met by scorn, suffering, and sometimes death, they held fast to the law revealed to Moses and the new covenant promises that were yet to come (Ezekiel 36:26–27), their hope in a future redeemer (Isaiah 59:20).

The gloomy end to the Old Testament shows God's people living in exile, suffering and scattered. The law of God, his precious words to his people, have been lost and forgotten. The temple has been destroyed. The kings are gone; the nation is broken. And yet there is still a note of hope. The law, once lost and forgotten, is rediscovered. This discovery brings renewed hope to a remnant of the people of God as they return from exile. One of the most powerful scenes in the Old Testament is found in the book of Nehemiah, when Ezra, the priest, stands to read the Book of the Law, a book that had somehow endured throughout the destruction:

> All the people came together as one in the square before the Water Gate. They told Ezra the teacher of the Law to bring out the Book of the Law of Moses, which the LORD had commanded for Israel.
>
> So on the first day of the seventh month Ezra the priest brought the Law before the assembly, which was made up of men and women and all who were able to understand. He read it aloud from daybreak till noon as he faced the square before the Water Gate in the presence of the men, women and others who could understand. And all the people listened attentively to the Book of the Law.
>
> Ezra the teacher of the Law stood on a high wooden platform built for the occasion ...
>
> Ezra opened the book. All the people could see him because he was standing above them; and as he opened it, the people all stood up. Ezra praised the LORD, the great God; and all the people lifted their hands and responded, "Amen! Amen!" Then they bowed down and worshiped the LORD with their faces to the ground.
>
> The Levites ... instructed the people in the Law while the people were standing there. They read from the Book of the Law of God, making it clear and giving the meaning so that the people understood what was being read.
>
> Then Nehemiah the governor, Ezra the priest and teacher of the Law, and the Levites who were instructing the people said to them all, "This day is holy to the LORD your God. Do not mourn or weep." For all the people had been weeping as they listened to the words of the Law.

> Nehemiah said, "Go and enjoy choice food and sweet drinks, and send some to those who have nothing prepared. This day is holy to our Lord. Do not grieve, for the joy of the LORD is your strength."
>
> The Levites calmed all the people, saying, "Be still, for this is a holy day. Do not grieve."
>
> Then all the people went away to eat and drink, to send portions of food and to celebrate with great joy, because they now understood the words that had been made known to them. **Nehemiah 8:1–12**

Israel returned from years of captivity and exile to a destroyed temple and city. No one had seen or heard God's law recorded by Moses for many years. And yet God preserved for his people his word, his covenant promises, and his revealed character through a few faithful kings, prophets, and scribes throughout the generations. He did this so that when the promised Messiah would come, his people would know and recognize him.

## The Messiah, Jesus

Sadly, when the Messiah finally came as the prophets had foretold, his people did *not* recognize him. In fact, their hard hearts and deaf ears led them to misunderstand who the Messiah was and what his purposes in deliverance were. Expecting a warrior-king who would destroy the Roman occupiers, they were not looking for a spiritual teacher who would be crucified on a cross. Jesus was a living example of what it means to guard and embody the truth of God. Jesus fulfilled all that the prophets had spoken and was the perfect sacrifice who saved his people from their sins (Matthew 1:21). Jesus was more than a steward of the truth; he *was* the truth (John 14:6). He was the Word made flesh, come to dwell among us (John 1:14).

Jesus came to affirm the law and all that the prophets had spoken, and he came to fulfill God's word. We learn this from Jesus' own words in the Sermon on the Mount (Matthew 5–7). Jesus spoke to the significance and role the law now has in the kingdom of God.[2] He came to usher in the kingdom of God (Mark 1:15) through his life, death, and resurrection. After his resurrection, in a conversation with two discouraged disciples on the road to Emmaus, Jesus explained his unique role in God's redemptive plan: " 'How foolish you are, and how slow to believe all that the prophets have spoken! Did not the Messiah have to suffer these things and then enter his glory?' And beginning with Moses and all the Prophets, he explained to them what was said in all the Scriptures concerning himself" (Luke 24:25–27).

In the midst of their confusion and discouragement, Jesus speaks to his disciples and reveals that he is the one whose person and work fulfill the truth proclaimed by Moses and the prophets throughout the ages. As the risen Savior, he now possesses all authority on heaven and earth (Matthew 28:18) to declare the truth about God, his covenant promises, and his plan of redemption.

## Guardians of the Gospel

Jesus soon ascends to his Father, but he leaves the apostles with the empowerment of the Holy Spirit and commends them as the sole stewards of the truth of the gospel. He commands them to be his witnesses on earth (Acts 1:8). In this role, the apostles commit their time and energy to "prayer and the ministry of the word" (6:4). The book of Acts contains the story of how the early church is built, recording the faithful stewardship of the apostles doing the very things Jesus has commanded them to do. We see how the Holy Spirit powerfully works in and through them. And we are introduced to the apostle Paul, a converted enemy of the church who has a significant role in raising up and training a new generation of leaders to guard the gospel truth.

In his letters to Timothy and Titus, Paul gives a summary of this call. To Timothy he writes, "Guard the good deposit that was entrusted to you" (2 Timothy 1:14). He instructs Timothy to guard the sound words—the doctrines that Paul has taught him—and to entrust them to reliable people (2:2). A key aspect of guarding the truth is this idea of preservation. Paul tells Timothy that one of the reasons his instruction is necessary is the sad fact that his closest friends and ministry partners have deserted him: "You know that everyone in the province of Asia has deserted me, including Phygelus and Hermogenes" (1:15). Paul was constantly facing opponents of the gospel, men and women who wished to distort the message. Nearing the end of his life, Paul understands it is necessary to pass on the gospel "deposit" to the next generation. He writes to Timothy, knowing that many of the same enemies of the gospel will confront Timothy as well.

This same command—to guard the gospel—is also seen in Paul's letter to the young pastor Titus. Paul writes to Titus and tells him to appoint godly, biblically qualified leaders in Crete (Titus 1:5) for the very same reasons he wrote to Timothy. Titus is commanded to appoint pastors (elders) in every city who "hold firmly to the trustworthy message as it has been taught," for the purpose of encouraging others with doctrine and refuting "those who oppose it" (1:9). Paul explains to Titus that these are men who will distort and oppose the trustworthy message of the gospel (1:10–16).

From these examples, we learn that guardians of the gospel of Jesus Christ have a twofold purpose: to *hold firmly* to the faithful word and to *refute* those who would contradict it. Pastors are the appointed guardians of God's truth, and above all else they must hold firm to it, boldly refuting those who come against it and passing it on to the next generation of appointed guardians.

Jesus came as the fulfillment of the law and the words of the prophets. And Jesus spoke his word to his apostles, and they wrote that word down and then spoke it to others—men like Timothy and Titus. Along with this word, they gave a special charge as well: to guard the truth of the gospel. The teaching of the apostles has now been passed down to us, from generation to generation over the past two thousand years, entrusted to faithful under-shepherds in every generation. And that brings us to you today. As a pastor and leader in the church, you belong to a long lineage of guardians, those entrusted to guard the deposit regardless of the cost and then to entrust it to the next generation. That's your calling, one of the priorities of your ministry as a pastor. But how, practically, do you do this?

## Guarding the Truth in Ministry

The gospel is the good news of Jesus. And it is good news *about* Jesus, the story of what God has done from beginning to end to create, save, and bless a people who are his own. It is the truth that God created everything good and perfect, and that through Adam and Eve, sin entered the world. Human sin affects everything now, including those created in God's image. Human beings are born into this world as sinners, cut off from God with no hope to save ourselves, no hope of being reconciled to God by our own efforts. The gospel is the good news that God in his mercy does not leave us in our hopeless condition, but sent his only Son, Jesus, to rescue us, redeem us, and restore us to relationship with God. Jesus came to earth, lived a perfect life, and died an atoning death on the cross for sinners, thus bearing the wrath of God in their place. Three days later, he rose from the grave, conquering death, and now sits at the right hand of the Father, ruling over the nations and waiting to return for his bride, the church. Anyone who turns from their sins, believes, and trusts in Jesus Christ alone by faith is rescued from the wrath to come, forgiven of all their sins, clothed in the righteousness of Jesus, and adopted as a child of the living God. All of this is a gift of God's grace. This is the truth of the gospel, and for nearly two thousand years this message has been entrusted to those who follow Christ—particularly pastors.

Pastors do more than speak the message of the gospel; they guard the *essential truths* of the gospel. Paul, in writing to his young disciples Timothy and Titus, is aware of the looming presence of false teachers, those who twist and distort the truth of the gospel. Like Timothy and Titus, we must be aware that a key part of our responsibility in guarding the truth of the gospel is making sure we understand it and that we declare certain key aspects of the message. We need to speak about the sinlessness of Jesus, the fully divine and fully human natures of Jesus, the substitutionary atonement of his death, the imputation of righteousness and reality of forgiveness for his followers, the physical resurrection of Jesus, and his rulership at the right hand of God.

We know there will always be people who speak against the truth of the gospel, who will try to distort it in some way, so our defense against these distortions is a primary responsibility of pastoral ministry. Yet in addition to guarding against these overt false teachings, a pastor in a typical evangelical church today faces two additional, even more subtle dangers. First, out of a desire to keep things simple or sometimes for rhetorical appeal, a pastor may leave out several important and essentials elements of the gospel. Simplicity is a good virtue, but we cannot sacrifice truth on the altar of simplicity and clarity. So even if something is hard to understand or requires a more complex explanation, we must take the time to teach it and explain it. Don't avoid the more difficult teachings of Scripture in an effort to keep things simple.

Second, it is possible for those who have been Christians for a long time to begin to *assume* the gospel. They may assume everyone knows it already (which is not true). Or they may think that once a person has heard and understood or responded to the gospel, there is no need to talk about it anymore. I once heard a pastor talk about the danger of assuming the gospel, and he said this: "A generation that assumes these essential elements about the gospel loses the gospel in the next generation."[3] So how do you keep your people from assuming the gospel? How do you encourage them to value and uphold the beauty of the gospel? Pastors guard the truth of the gospel by *regularly* proclaiming it among God's people and then winsomely *applying* it to life through the weekly preaching of God's word. Don't assume the gospel; preach it regularly. We protect the truth when we speak about it, when we pass it on to others, and when we show how the truth of the gospel continues to apply to the daily concerns of life. When we fail to do this, we fail to guard the gospel. The gospel's power in our church and in our own lives will be weakened.

## Defend the Authority of All Scripture

The gospel is the good news of Jesus, which reveals how the redemptive plan of God throughout history culminates in the coming of Jesus. And as essential as it is to guard the gospel message, this doesn't mean we should neglect the other teachings of Scripture that relate to and flow out of the gospel. We need to uphold the sound words of the apostles' teaching, and this means teaching on the entirety of Scripture—what we know as the Old and New Testaments. Paul writes that "all Scripture is God-breathed," indicating it is inspired by God, and Paul adds that it "is useful for teaching, rebuking, correcting and training in righteousness" (2 Timothy 3:16). In his letter to the Corinthian church, Paul refers to the Hebrew Scriptures (our Old Testament), noting that the examples of Israel's disobedience "were written down as warnings for us" (1 Corinthians 10:11). Guarding the truth means recognizing that we need to instruct from the Old and New Testaments. The *whole* counsel of God is God's authoritative, inerrant, infallible word. Let me offer three suggestions on how a pastor can do this.

First, as you plan your preaching, make it your goal to preach through entire books of the Bible. While there is a place for topical preaching, one of the problems with it is that it allows a pastor to avoid dealing with hard texts. Topical preaching allows a pastor to choose the texts he wants to refer to in addressing a specific issue and thus avoid controversial or challenging passages. But if you are committed to preaching through books of the Bible and your people know it is your commitment, you cannot dance around difficult passages. Preaching through entire books provides a balanced diet of biblical exposition for your church, and at the same time it defends the authority and value of the whole Bible.

Second, following the intent of the last suggestion, try to preach and teach a balance of the Old *and* New Testament in your church. If the overwhelming majority of a pastor's sermons come from the New Testament year after year, a message is communicated to the congregation that the Old Testament isn't as important as the New Testament, and they will not value the Old Testament as useful for teaching and training in righteousness. The need for balance can be extended even further, making sure a balance of genres and sections is preached as well. For example, if most of a pastor's sermons are pulled from Paul's letters and rarely from the Gospels, a congregation may conclude that Paul's words are more important than those of Jesus. A steady and balanced diet of both Old and New Testaments and the various genres within them is critical.

One of the ways we have tried to strike this balance in our church is to preach from different Testaments in the morning and evening services. At times, we have even tried to take the passage from the morning sermon and select a passage from the other Testament for the evening that somehow connects with the morning passage. We also try to vary genres between the two Testaments. Though that balance is off at times, the goal is to uphold the whole of the Bible before our people so they understand that *all* of it is profitable for teaching, correction, and training.

Third, if you aren't rotating your preaching between the Old and New Testaments, at least try to have a reading from both the Old and New Testaments in every gathering for worship. This has historically been the practice of the church, and this balanced approach allows a service planner to show how the Bible fits together as one book—one redemptive story. These simple efforts, done well over time, will effectively train people in understanding their Bible and in coming to cherish all of it as a gift from God. In doing this, pastors teach their people how to guard the truth.

Finally, apply this principle to the Bible studies, small groups, Sunday school classes, and other group meetings in which God's word is taught by others. For example, consider making adjustments if you find that most of your small groups land in Paul's letters by default. Or provide a few biblical book studies in your Sunday school classes if you tend to gravitate toward topical issues. Evaluate your patterns within children and youth ministries and the biblical instruction provided there as well. Defending the authority of all of Scripture begins in the pulpit, but it takes deep root in a church when a pastor leads in this evaluation of all the church's ministries. *I should have final say over all* *teaching ministries*

## Pursue Cultural Awareness

Every generation of Christian pastors has had to apply the truth of the gospel to their own unique context and culture. So it is essential that a pastor understands the culture he is called to minister to if he wants to be effective in communicating truth. Modern technology, social media, and the rise of secularization have made this even more essential today. One of today's most respected cultural Christian commentators, Dr. Albert Mohler, once told a group of pastors, "We're watching in one generation the collapse of cultural Christianity ... and it's coming with a new velocity and a new intensity. What is now being mandated as morally right wasn't even morally mentionable a generation ago ... In short order we are going to find out what it's like to be on the underside of society, rather than the upside."[4]

Mohler's warning highlights our need as guardians of truth to know our culture well. This involves engaging in opportunities to grow in our cultural awareness. Pastors need to study, but they should study and read *broadly*. Pastors should try to stay up on the current events and the latest cultural news. They need to be aware of what is happening in our academic institutions, be informed about upcoming political elections, and have their pulse on the moral controversies of our day. Obviously, they can't be an expert on everything. But they need to have a basic knowledge of the world in which they live so they can respond with wisdom. Pastors must be informed so they know *how* to guard the truth and can effectively disciple their flock to guard the truth. Apologetics is not simply knowing how to share the gospel; it requires some knowledge of modern heresies and cultural barriers to the gospel. A pastor who understands the culture is better equipped to guard the truth and to teach others to do the same.

## Watch Over the Flock

In addition to providing public biblical instruction as a means of guarding doctrine, pastors and church leaders must guard the truth by exercising discipline as they exhort people to the true practice of their faith. Peter exhorts pastors to watch over the flock as a function of shepherding (1 Peter 5:2), and this means a pastor is to oversee that God's word is taught and preached and that it serves as the standard for the practice of the church in its day-to-day operations. Although often disconnected from the call of shepherding, this task is a key component of guarding the truth. Though some of this responsibility is delegated to other church leaders (deacons and other leaders), ultimately those who are pastors must maintain oversight over the entire church.

Pastors watch over the flock as they administrate. This includes caring for souls, equipping leaders, discipling members, reaching the lost through evangelistic efforts, and being stewards of the church's resources. In large churches, a pastor cannot meet one-on-one with everyone in the church on a regular basis, but he can appoint other mature Christians to meet with two or three other members in the church and report back to the pastors on how these meetings are going. In these situations, the pastor is still watching over the flock, though not directly meeting with everyone in the church.

Pastoral oversight is also needed in the administrative, financial, logistical, and organizational aspects of church life. There are services that need to be planned every week. There are finances to manage, facilities to maintain, staff to supervise, and other leaders to raise up and train. Many pastors avoid these responsibilities or don't want anything to do with this side of church life. Others spend too much time in these areas, neglecting the preaching of the word. It's easy for administrative tasks to eat up great amounts of a pastor's time every week. Exercising oversight means finding the right balance between wisely handing off responsibilities to faithful servants, yet being aware of and in touch with what is happening in the church. In our church, I have nothing to do with counting the offerings on Sundays, nor am I informed about what every member gives. Yet every month, before we share financial details with the church body, I review our monthly financial statement so I am aware of our financial numbers and how the money was spent that month. I have enough information to ask questions, and I understand the general financial condition of our church, yet much of the day-to-day work in this area is carried out by others. This allows me to be involved in unusual or unexpected financial decision making when needed, but it frees me up for other responsibilities.

To watch over the flock means we must be *biblically minded* in our calling, yet *practically minded* in how we apply biblical principles in the administration of the church. Pastors must be organized in wise, efficient, and creative ways so they have a working knowledge of every area in the church without getting bogged down with the day-to-day operations. As a pastor, you guard the truth, not just by watching your life and doctrine, but by operating with wisdom in overseeing all aspects of church life.

## Conclusion

A close friend became a pastor at a small, struggling historic congregation in the southeastern part of the United States.

Although the church was struggling, it had a rich heritage. Decades earlier, it had been a vibrant local church and a gospel light in its community. This pastor accepted the call knowing the rich biblical heritage, yet he was also aware of the decades of dysfunction and unaware of the precise cause. After beginning his ministry, he researched the church's history and traced the internal conflicts, financial struggles, and heretical teachings back to a single source—a string of unfaithful shepherds. Over the course of several decades, the church had a string of pastors with patterns of moral failings, dictator-style leadership, financial dishonesty, theological ambiguity, and, most apparent of all, a lack of clarity with regard to the gospel and a lack of commitment to the Scriptures as the word of God. Within two generations, unfaithful shepherds not committed to guarding the truth had caused the church to crumble.

This church is an example of what happens when leaders abandon their commitment to guard the truth, yet this church is also a positive example, a testimony to the power of God and the Scriptures. Under the leadership of their new pastor, this once dying and dysfunctional church began to thrive again. It didn't happen immediately, but after a decade of solid, biblical teaching and faithful gospel ministry the church is once again a light in the community. People are walking in the truth, and lives are being transformed. My friend would quickly say this new life is not due to particular strategies, trendy programs, or his own leadership charisma; it is the fruit of God's word bringing new spiritual life. And though he hopes to have several more years of fruitful ministry in this place, he is already mindful of his top priority—to raise up a new generation who will guard the truth that has been rediscovered and reclaimed in this church.

Today, nearly two thousand years after Christ's ascension, Christ's church has been established throughout the world. And by God's grace, it will continue to grow and expand as faithful men are entrusted with the truth and raise up the next generation do to the same. A pastor's primary, instinctive calling must be to guard the good deposit and entrust that truth to other reliable men. The priorities of a pastor's life and ministry can be filled with many good labors, but all of these must be grounded in and driven by the stewardship of the truth of God, the gospel of Jesus, and the whole of Scripture. If pastors and church leaders fail to do this, they will end up building their lives and ministries on things that will not last. If we lose the truth, we have nothing left. But if we guard the truth and make it the lifeblood of our ministry, we labor in the work that the Spirit empowers and through which he breathes life to our souls and the souls of our people.

## Chapter 2

# Preach the Word

In the presence of God and of Christ Jesus, who will
judge the living and the dead, and in view of his
appearing and his kingdom, I give you this charge:
Preach the word; be prepared in season and out of
season; correct, rebuke and encourage — with great
patience and careful instruction.          2 Timothy 4:1–2

Time to study in preparation for preaching often gets squeezed out of a pastor's busy schedule. Yet amid the competing demands of ministry, the study and preaching of the word of God should be the central focus of every faithful pastor's ministry. In recent years, as busy pastors utilize changes in technology and the wealth of resources available on the Internet, an interesting dynamic called "sermon plagiarism" has developed — the temptation to make use of immediately accessible information, borrowing outlines or in some cases word-for-word manuscripts from other pastors and preaching them to the congregation. Pastors who lack a message for their Sunday message can take the sermons of popular, gifted, and successful pastors and easily claim them as their own. Adding to this temptation is the encouragement of some preachers to do this as a matter of convenience, with the intent of freeing busy pastors so they can focus on other responsibilities. One well-known pastor boldly says other pastors should utilize his work to enhance their own ministry: "Use them."[5] And elsewhere he says, "When I was planting Saddleback Church, other pastors' sermons fed my soul — and eased my preparation!

I hope [my] sermons ... will do the same for you. Whether you use the outlines and transcripts for sermon ideas or listen to the preaching to fine-tune your delivery, I'll be thrilled if your ministry becomes more effective."[6]

To be clear, Pastor Rick Warren's generosity and his desire to help other pastors are commendable. Ultimately, however, it is shortsighted and unwise to encourage this type of behavior. Why? Because a pastor is called to *preach*. And that involves study. It involves personal reflection on the word. It involves meditation and prayer. There are no shortcuts or substitutes for these things. A pastor is not just called to preach God's word, but to preach a word that has been deeply internalized and appropriately applied to his people.

I want to do more than simply affirm the importance of preaching; I want to commend a particular *process of preparing* to preach. Paul tells Timothy in 2 Timothy 4 that part of preaching the word is being prepared for that work, and I believe preparation necessarily involves a commitment to study and prayer—a process that cannot be substituted with the work of another person. While the sermons of other pastors can be helpful when used appropriately, preparing to preach involves a definite commitment of a pastor's heart and time. Without that commitment, a pastor's public ministry of the word of God will never be all that it can be, nor will it be what God designed it to be.

## A Biblical Command: Preach

Throughout the pages of Scripture God speaks to his people through an appointed leader. God speaks and seeks a response from his people. In the Old Testament, God chooses a nation—Israel—from among the other nations to be his special people. Israel failed to respond to this word as God desired, turning away in sin and idolatry, yet this pattern of God speaking through mediators and calling for a response, would remain consistent throughout the story line of Scripture.

## Israel

When the descendants of Jacob were enslaved by the Egyptians, God listened to the cries of his people in Egypt and rescued them from their slavery. Moses became God's appointed leader, and he was responsible to bring God's word to the people. God made a covenant with his people through the mediation of Moses, who declared God's word to the people. The people responded in agreement. Here is the scene as this covenant (known as the "old covenant") between God and Israel is made:

> Then the LORD said to Moses, "Come up to the LORD, you and Aaron, Nadab and Abihu, and seventy of the elders of Israel. You are to worship at a distance, but Moses alone is to approach the LORD; the others must not come near. And the people may not come up with him."
>
> When Moses went and told the people all the LORD's words and laws, they responded with one voice, "Everything the LORD has said we will do." Moses then wrote down everything the LORD had said.
>
> He got up early the next morning and built an altar at the foot of the mountain and set up twelve stone pillars representing the twelve tribes of Israel. Then he sent young Israelite men, and they offered burnt offerings and sacrificed young bulls as fellowship offerings to the LORD. Moses took half of the blood and put it in bowls, and the other half he splashed against the altar. Then he took the Book of the Covenant and read it to the people. They responded, "We will do everything the LORD has said; we will obey."
>
> Moses then took the blood, sprinkled it on the people and said, "This is the blood of the covenant that the LORD has made with you in accordance with all these words." **Exodus 24:1 – 8**

Notice that the people and the elders are not allowed into God's presence. Instead, they need someone to represent them and mediate God's word to them. God's design is to communicate his word through an appointed leader (Moses), who will hear that word from God and deliver it to the people. The people respond to the word with one voice, declaring they will obey (Exodus 24:7).

Despite the faithfulness of God, the people do not obey; they rebel. Yet God continues speaking to his people through appointed leaders who speak his word, always calling for a response to that word. This pattern is seen throughout the ministry of the prophets. The prophets remind the people of God's law, his covenant with them, and they let the people know God calls them to repent and turn back to him. Again, the people reject that word, yet the appointed mouthpieces of the Lord remain faithful to speak what God has revealed for them. Many of them suffer and are persecuted because of their obedience.

Israel's history has a few glimpses of the people's obedience to the word, foreshadowing God's future redemption of his people. King David responds in repentance to God's word that comes through the prophet Nathan (2 Samuel 12). And there is no doubt many of the psalmists had a deep love for God's word, and some people obeyed their calls to love and obey God's word. The beauty, length, and content of Psalm 119 alone remind us that portions of God's people within the nation of Israel loved the law of the Lord and sought not just to obey it but to delight in and meditate on it as well.

Arguably, the most powerful Old Testament picture of God speaking to his people and bringing them life through his word is found in the prophet Ezekiel's vision in a valley of dry bones:

> The hand of the LORD was on me, and he brought me out by the Spirit of the LORD and set me in the middle of a valley; it was full of bones. He led me back and forth among them, and I saw a great many bones

on the floor of the valley, bones that were very dry. He asked me, "Son of man, can these bones live?"

I said, "Sovereign LORD, you alone know."

Then he said to me, "Prophesy to these bones and say to them, 'Dry bones, hear the word of the LORD! This is what the Sovereign LORD says to these bones: I will make breath enter you, and you will come to life. I will attach tendons to you and make flesh come upon you and cover you with skin; I will put breath in you, and you will come to life. Then you will know that I am the LORD.'"

So I prophesied as I was commanded. And as I was prophesying, there was a noise, a rattling sound, and the bones came together, bone to bone. I looked, and tendons and flesh appeared on them and skin covered them, but there was no breath in them.

Then he said to me, "Prophesy to the breath; prophesy, son of man, and say to it, 'This is what the Sovereign LORD says: Come, breath, from the four winds and breathe into these slain, that they may live.'" So I prophesied as he commanded me, and breath entered them; they came to life and stood up on their feet — a vast army.                    **Ezekiel 37:1 – 10**

This is a powerful picture of how God brings life to his people. God speaks through his mouthpiece to dead and lifeless people, and the word through his Spirit brings life. In this vision the Sovereign Lord reveals his divine design to breathe life into his people, a plan that is accomplished in the new covenant promises secured by the blood of Jesus Christ.

## The Church

The long-awaited Messiah, Jesus Christ, is the one who inaugurates a new covenant. Through his perfect life, death, and resurrection, Jesus purchases with his own blood a people for himself. Unlike Israel, these redeemed people have God's Spirit placed in them and God's word written on their hearts so they are able to obey God's word (Ezekiel 36:26–27). God's people are now able to hear his word through his appointed servants and respond in obedience. The church depends on the preaching of God's word for its life.

On the day of Pentecost we see how the Holy Spirit comes on God's messengers in a powerful way (Acts 2:1–4). With the pouring out of the Spirit, the church is birthed, and we see on full display God's fulfillment of his plan to build his kingdom. God's appointed messenger, the apostle Peter, preaches the gospel (Acts 2:14–36) and calls his hearers to respond to God's word about Jesus (Acts 2:37–40). The people respond in repentance, faith, and willingness to be baptized (Acts 2:41–42). The apostolic preaching of the word of God in the power of the Holy Spirit is the means by which God builds his church.

As the apostles pass on the torch to the next generation, the pattern set by the apostles is continued. Pastors of local churches continue preaching the apostolic witness for the establishment, growth, and health of the people of God. Paul's letters to Timothy and Titus reveal the importance of the ministry of the word. Paul exhorts Timothy to guard the good deposit of the gospel and sound teaching from God's word, for it has been entrusted to him. And as we saw in the last chapter, one of the primary ways this deposit is guarded is through the preaching of the word: "In the presence of God and of Christ Jesus, who will judge the living and the dead, and in view of his appearing and his kingdom, I give you this charge: Preach the word; be prepared in season and out of season; correct, rebuke and encourage—with great patience and careful instruction" (2 Timothy 4:1–2).

God's divine design throughout the ages to build his kingdom of redeemed people culminates in this powerful charge: "Preach the word." Paul explains how, when, and why a pastor is to preach the word and that it should be done with the patience and precision of a gifted, called shepherd of the Lord Jesus Christ. Pastors are entrusted to care for the souls of people as men who will give an account (Hebrews 13:17). The apostles knew a lot was at stake. They took seriously their responsibility to teach and to train a new generation of pastors who would accept the mantle from them. Paul writes to Timothy, emphasizing the importance of holding to the truth and teaching it to others:

> Until I come, devote yourself to the public reading of Scripture, to preaching and to teaching. Do not neglect your gift, which was given you through prophecy when the body of elders laid their hands on you.
> Be diligent in these matters; give yourself wholly to them, so that everyone may see your progress.
> Watch your life and doctrine closely. Persevere in them, because if you do, you will save both yourself and your hearers.            **1 Timothy 4:13–16**

This charge, while applicable in some sense to all believers, is specially given to Spirit-filled, gifted men who are biblically qualified pastors (1 Timothy 3:1–7). They are called to preach the word to the people they shepherd, to live that word, and to call people to respond to the gospel.

Even though we live in a different time and culture, the fact remains that God's church is built this same way today. The Pastoral Epistles outline a detailed template for preaching and how this builds the church. Pastors must study and prepare themselves so they can hear God's word. A pastor internalizes that word and then preaches it to the people by the Spirit, calling his particular people to respond in obedience. This is more than a human activity; it is a divinely designed spiritual experience between a pastor and his congregation. And the work of preparation is an essential component. It does not happen when a pastor preaches another's sermons or skimps on the work of preparation. The heart work is key as well, and it is well worth the investment of time as it bears spiritual fruit.

## How to Preach like a Shepherd

A preacher can preach several types of sermons: doctrinal messages, which focus on a particular doctrine such as election, sin, perseverance, Scripture, ecclesiology, and eschatology; evangelistic messages, which communicate the gospel and call the unconverted to believe in Christ; and topical messages, which address a certain topic or felt need in the congregation. None of these are bad in themselves, and all have their place at some point. Yet to ensure that God's people are consistently exposed to the word of God, the best way to preach faithfully and accurately is to preach *expository* sermons.

An expository sermon flows from and is built completely on a text from Scripture, not on an idea, a doctrine, an event, or a topic. To help visualize this, imagine a stack of building blocks where the bottom foundational block is a text of Scripture. In building an expository message, every block you place in the sermon is built on this block. Expository preaching functions best when pastors preach passage by passage through different books of the Bible.

I have three reasons for believing expository sermons are the most helpful and faithful way for a pastor to feed his people regularly:

*1. Expository sermons affirm the authority, power, and sufficiency of Scripture.* As I mentioned in the last chapter, a pastor cannot avoid the hard passages when he preaches expository sermons. When I was preaching through 2 Samuel in my local church, I preached on David's adultery and murder one week, and rape, incest, and murder among David's children the next week—passages I would not have chosen to preach on if I were randomly picking a passage for the week. Yet our people need to hear what God is saying through these passages, and we as pastors need to wrestle with them to understand what God wants us to learn from them. Preach the hard passages. If your congregation sees you are not afraid to wrestle with them, then they will surely grow less afraid of them too.

*2. Expository sermons help our people know how to read their Bibles as intended*. A pastor and his people will come to better understand the meaning of each book or section of Scripture. I am always amazed at how much better I understand a writer's intent after preaching through the natural flow of his argument or narrative. For example, when I was preaching on David's adultery, I saw how it linked back to David's acceptance of a second wife in 1 Samuel. This was not something I read in a commentary; it came to me through following the narrative's progression as I preached through this Bible book. It is difficult to see connections like this unless a pastor spends time poring over the passage week after week. *I totally agree. ⌐*

*3. Expository sermons help keep a pastor focused on preaching God's words instead of human words*. Expository sermons on entire books of the Bible provide a fruitful and steady diet for a church. This type of preaching also teaches listeners how to read their Bibles. When we commit to preaching through books of the Bible, not picking and choosing what we want to read or study, we teach our people to do the same on their own.

## Preach Your Own Material

While not every pastor is tempted to preach someone else's sermons, most rely on the opinions, insights, and scholarly wisdom of others found in commentaries, language tools, and theological writings. Let's face it; we live in a blessed time! We have easy access to the thoughts of some of the most brilliant theological minds in history, and we can see what they think about almost any passage in the Bible. With access to these kinds of scholars, the temptation we face is to rely on the thoughts and insights of others before formulating our own thoughts about the passage. What is the balance here? When should a preacher consult the scholars, and when should he go with his own insights?

The words of the nineteenth-century English pastor Andrew Fuller are just as sound in our commentary-saturated time as they were in his day when resources were scarce. Fuller wrote this in a letter to a young pastor:

> The method I pursued was, first to read the text carefully over, and as I went on, to note down what first struck me as the meaning. After reducing these notes into something like a scheme of the passage, I examined the best experts I could procure, and, comparing my own first thoughts with theirs, was better able to judge of their justness. Some of them were confirmed, some corrected, and many added to them ... But to go first to expositors is to preclude the exercise of your own judgment.[7]

Pastors, we need to be grateful for the abundance of commentaries and theological writings we have available to us. Use them! Let them confirm and even correct your own thoughts *after* you have done your own study. But guard yourself from relying too heavily on them. Busy pastors are frequently tempted to take the path of least resistance and preach the thoughts of others instead of doing the hard work of allowing the Spirit of the living God to work that text in us as a word that will speak specifically to our flock. Authentic, biblical, Spirit-filled preaching happens when a preacher has been deeply impacted by a passage, and it is just as necessary today as it was in Fuller's day.

### Preach with Your People in Mind

The task of preaching is more than just preaching the word; it involves carefully and wisely applying that word to the lives of the people entrusted to your care. As you prepare to preach God's word, you should have your people on your mind. Think about the difficulties they are facing, the challenges in their lives right now. How does God's word from this passage minister grace to them? Ask questions like, "How does this truth relate to Joe's marriage? How does this characteristic of God speak to the pain Margaret is feeling after losing her husband? How does this passage help Sarah care for her home more faithfully, help Doug deal with his difficult boss, or minister grace to Sally, who just found out she has cancer? A pastor should have specific people on his mind to help him apply the truth of God's word directly to the unique situations in his congregation.

Another way to be considerate and conscious of your people is to think through *how long* you should preach. Biblically, there is no specified time for a message. So the length should be determined by several factors, largely affected by your cultural context and the spiritual needs of your people. First, consider the spiritual maturity of your people—where they actually are, not where you think they should be. We should always challenge our folks to grow, yet I hear of pastors who preach long sermons, knowing full well they overwhelm the majority of their congregation. Their reason is that they are pushing their people, stretching them so they can listen to God's word for the amount of time the pastor *thinks* is appropriate. By all means, push your congregation to grow, but don't exasperate them or kill their love for the word by preaching long sermons they can't handle. God must do his work. Preach faithfully, but meet them where they are. Let God mature them to the place they need to be. Your preaching should lead them to long for more, not to wish you had ended sooner.

The length of a message should also be based on your own abilities and skill. Be honest; how good and seasoned a preacher are you? I tend to spend time with other pastors who love to read the Puritans, and when you read that these men preached one- to two-hour sermons, it's tempting to think, *Hey, I want to be like the Puritans*. But the honest truth is that many who want to preach for an hour are not yet good enough or seasoned enough to preach for a full hour. Each pastor needs to honestly evaluate his own preaching. If you have trouble with this, get some input from those you trust. Ask your wife. Ask a friend or a trusted elder. Be ready to hear their honest feedback, and receive it as an invitation to grow and learn. If you are in your first year of pastoring a church, your sermons will probably need to be shorter and simpler than you probably think they should be.

Lastly, as I briefly mentioned above, remember that it is good to leave your people longing for more, not less. Every preacher has been there. You sense you are losing people—and you still have ten minutes left in your sermon. Give adequate time to the preaching of God's word, but try to leave your listeners longing for more when you end. I would rather leave my people in a place where they wanted a little more, where they look forward to coming back next week, than overloading them to the point where they can't wait to leave. When someone is thirsty for a big glass of water, jamming a fire hose down their throat will quench their thirst, but it isn't a pleasant experience—nor is it one they'll want to repeat.

Remember you aren't just a voice mechanically communicating a message; you are a shepherd of God's people. Think like a shepherd. Push your people to grow, but do it wisely. Nurture them by meeting them where they are. Then trust that God will use his word and your efforts to find a balance than encourages growth.

## Preach with Yourself in Mind

In 1 Timothy 4:16, the apostle Paul urges Timothy to "watch your life and doctrine closely." A preacher of God's word will not have the same impact on his people if he has not first been deeply affected by the word. The nineteenth-century English pastor Archibald Brown understood this as he spoke to his congregation:

> Oh, brethren and sisters, I would to God I could speak to you this morning as I would. I only wish I could make this text blaze away before your eyes as it has before my own. I would that its tremendous force might be realized by you, as it has been felt in my own heart before coming here. Oh, how it would shake some of you out of your selfishness, out of your worldliness, out of your pandering to the maxims of this world.[8]

Brown's words capture an essential element of powerful preaching: *A preacher must be deeply affected by the word he steps*

48

*into the pulpit to preach.* Before he can persuade a sinner to turn to Christ, he must first be persuaded himself. Before a preacher can convince fellow Christians to trust in the promises of God, he must first believe those promises. Pastors cannot be changed *by* the word unless they spend time *in* the word as they prepare to preach. It is essential that every pastor preaching God's word makes sure this word is a part of him and that he truly believes what he has prepared to preach. This heart preparation gives his preaching an earnestness that only comes from meeting with God and experiencing his help.

This help only comes through the work of the Holy Spirit. A pastor should first realize his own inability to preach powerfully and faithfully apart from the work of the Spirit. Gifted, eloquent pastors are tempted to rely on their own gifts and abilities when they stand before their people to preach. But every pastor, regardless of their own gifts or abilities, must realize that the power in their preaching comes from rightly handling the word of God through the Holy Spirit. A. W. Tozer cuts through much of the superficial and cultural emphasis of our day in regard to preaching with these insightful words:

> Let me shock you at this point. A naturally bright person can carry on religious activity without a special gift from God. Filling church pulpits every week are some who are using only natural abilities and special training. Some are known as Bible expositors, for it is possible to read and study commentaries and then repeat what has been learned about the Scriptures. Yes, it may shock you, but it is true that anyone able to talk fluently can learn to use religious phrases and can become recognized as a preacher.
>
> But if any person is determined to preach so that his work and ministry will abide in the day of the judgment fire, then he must preach, teach, and exhort with the kind of love and concern that comes only through a genuine gift of the Holy Spirit—something beyond his own capabilities.[9]

A pastor's intellect, gifts, training, and speaking ability are all helpful in the preaching task, but they do not make one a powerful, Spirit-filled preacher. Powerful preaching comes through a work of the Spirit when God stirs the pastor's own heart, and a love for his people and the souls of men rise as his greatest burden.

Modern pastors should heed Paul's words to "watch your life and doctrine" through diligent study and preparation to preach. This means not just thinking about the best way to communicate to people, but also about preaching to our own hearts. A pastor's greatest asset when preaching the word is not a sharp mind or smooth eloquence, but rather a humble and contrite heart before the Lord, relying on the Holy Spirit to do its work.

## Conclusion

God builds his church and his kingdom through his appointed messengers who speak God's word. This is how the church was birthed, and it is how God will continue to build the modern church to display his glory. God builds his church, and he does it by his Spirit breathing life into the church through his life-giving word. A pastor's task is to preach the word with deep passion because his own mind, heart, and soul have been moved by it throughout his preparation. He is to prepare the message with his own unique group of people on his mind, thinking of how to speak this life-giving word into their lives. He is to proclaim God's word as if life and death, heaven and hell, hang in the balance. Pastors, make it your aim to guard the good deposit entrusted to you until the Chief Shepherd returns, passing on that deposit to the next generation.

## Chapter 3

# Pray for the Flock

> Pray in the Spirit on all occasions with all kinds of
> prayers and requests. With this in mind, be alert and
> always keep on praying for all the Lord's people.
>
> **Ephesians 6:18**

When I became a senior pastor, transitioning from an associate role at another church, my life and ministry suddenly became very busy—busier than they had ever been before. I knew, without a doubt, what I was called to do. I knew what I should be doing. Yet week after week, I saw the things I was supposed to be doing getting squeezed out of my schedule because of the urgent demands on my time. Above all else, the one task that was most neglected was prayer. And I don't think I'm alone in this. More than any other aspect of a pastor's calling, prayer is the most difficult to maintain. Prayer requires time. And prayer is usually most fruitful when done in a quiet place, without constant interruption or distraction. Unfortunately, prayer doesn't demand our attention. In the midst of people wanting our time and urgent tasks needing to be completed, spending time in prayer is easy to disregard.

A pastor knows he will be preaching every seven days, regardless of how busy he gets. The sermon must get done, and so time is set aside to fulfill that task. And sick people go to the hospital, and their suffering sits on your conscience so that even if you're busy, you'll eventually make the time to go. A death suddenly occurs and a funeral service must be prepared, and a pastor is at the mercy of the plans of that family and funeral home. Church leadership meetings get planned in advance, and these become default priorities in a pastor's schedule. Besides, other people are depending on him to be there and lead. But none of this is true with prayer. Prayer may sit on your conscience, but it isn't complaining. It remains on the list of tasks for the day, but those who are not prayed for are unaware that they are forgotten. As other demands steal our attention, prayer gets pushed to the background. Many pastors, myself included, will go week after week until eventually that soft but necessary voice calling us to stop and pray just fades out. If enough time passes, the voice of conviction and desire will go away. When that happens, prayer gets squeezed out of our life. Ironically, a pastor can be so busy caring for his people that he never makes time to stop and pray for them.

But this isn't right. It reveals a lack of faith and a problem with misplaced priorities. In fact, the aim of this chapter is to turn up the volume on that soft voice sitting on your conscience, that voice you often ignore in the midst of a busy life of ministry. My goal is not to shame you or manipulate you into praying. No, I trust that God's Spirit through his word will do the necessary work of convicting you and increasing your desire to pray. I only hope to turn up the volume by highlighting a theme that occurs all throughout Scripture. You see, you are uniquely called by God to come before God on behalf of your people and plead with God to work and move among your people—a calling to intercede for them. This is a theme that culminates in the perfect mediating work of Jesus Christ. We'll see how this is a consistent biblical pattern for God's leaders, and afterward, I'll mention some practical things that I hope will better equip you to pray for your flock. These are tools to help bring much-needed discipline to your life and ministry, restoring prayer to its proper place.

## The Need for an Intercessor

As I mentioned in chapter 1, God created the world, and it was all good and perfect (Genesis 1–2). Yet when Adam and Eve sinned against God and sin entered the world (Genesis 3), everything changed. One lasting implication is the relational separation between God and those he had created in his image. Yet God had a plan, and his plan was to reconcile his creation from the separation caused by sin. Repeatedly, God utilizes appointed leaders of his people to serve as intercessors for his people. An intercessor is simply one who pleads to God on behalf of others. This pattern reveals God's design for the pastoral role in the local church, but even more significantly, it reveals the gospel — that we are reconciled to God through the mediating (going-between) and intercessory (pleading on behalf of) work of the Redeemer — Jesus Christ.

### Moses on Behalf of Israel

God spoke to Abram and promised that a great nation would come from his offspring (Genesis 15). God was true to that promise and in his appointed time, the future generations of Abraham's offspring multiplied and formed a great nation — Israel. One of the most significant leaders of God's people was Moses, who was appointed by God to lead his people and play a mediating role between Israel and God. Moses' intercessory role is captured powerfully after Moses led the people out of bondage in Egypt and they built a golden calf and embraced idolatry. Then God became really angry:

> Then the LORD said to Moses, "Go down, because your people, whom you brought up out of Egypt, have become corrupt. They have been quick to turn away from what I commanded them and have made themselves an idol cast in the shape of a calf. They have bowed down to it and sacrificed to it and have said,

'These are your gods, Israel, who brought you up out of Egypt.'

"I have seen these people," the LORD said to Moses, "and they are a stiff-necked people. Now leave me alone so that my anger may burn against them and that I may destroy them. Then I will make you into a great nation."

But Moses sought the favor of the LORD his God. "LORD," he said, "why should your anger burn against your people, whom you brought out of Egypt with great power and a mighty hand? Why should the Egyptians say, 'It was with evil intent that he brought them out, to kill them in the mountains and to wipe them off the face of the earth'? Turn from your fierce anger; relent and do not bring disaster on your people. Remember your servants Abraham, Isaac and Israel, to whom you swore by your own self: 'I will make your descendants as numerous as the stars in the sky and I will give your descendants all this land I promised them, and it will be their inheritance forever.'" Then the LORD relented and did not bring on his people the disaster he had threatened.                        **Exodus 32:7 – 14**

God had just miraculously delivered his people and how did they show their gratefulness? They committed idolatry by worshiping a golden calf. No wonder the anger of the Lord burned against them, and he desired to destroy them (Exodus 32:10). And yet it was Moses who passionately cried out to the Lord on their behalf, begging God to show mercy (verses 11 – 13). As a result, the Lord relented and did not destroy them (verse 14). Moses interceded on behalf of God's people, and the Lord showed mercy.

However, Moses was neither a perfect leader nor a perfect mediator and intercessor. Israel was known for their pattern of disobedience to the Lord, and it would continue. Even in the midst of the people's failures, sins, and disobedience, the Lord remained faithful to his covenant and kept seeking to communicate with them through Moses and other future leaders who cried out to God on behalf of God's people.

### King David the Intercessor

A king rules over his people for the benefit of the people. King David was God's appointed king over his chosen people, Israel. David was not just God's appointed king; he was the one with whom God made another covenant — the Davidic covenant in which God promises David that he will raise up his descendant after him. This Son of David will rule over his kingdom — an everlasting kingdom that will never pass away (2 Samuel 7:12–16).

As God's appointed leader, David would go to God on behalf of his people, secure in the knowledge of this covenant promise that now existed between God and his chosen people and king. Although David was an imperfect king who even sinned grievously against the Lord (2 Samuel 11–12), David demonstrated a faithfulness to rule over God's people and plead for the Lord's blessing, presence, and care on them.

The psalms are full of examples of King David's role as the people's advocate to praise God for his goodness to them, plead for his forgiveness of their disobedience, and ask for the Lord's protection against their enemies. Here is one example:

The LORD is my strength and my shield;
　　my heart trusts in him, and he helps me.
My heart leaps for joy,
　　and with my song I praise him.
The LORD is the strength of his people,
　　a fortress of salvation for his anointed one.
*Save your people and bless your inheritance;*
　　*be their shepherd and carry them forever.*

　　　　　　　　　　　　　　**Psalm 28:7–9, italics added**

David was not a perfect king. Nevertheless, he possessed the character and qualities that show why he was God's chosen king. David trusted in the Lord. David knew the Lord would protect him and his people. David knew his God was sovereign over all his enemies. David relied on the Lord for strength for himself and for his people. David knew the Lord would save them and be their shepherd (Psalm 28:8–9). Because of this, David cried out to the Lord for help, pleading with the Lord on behalf of his people to save and rescue them (verse 9). David praised the Lord on behalf of his people. Although imperfect, David modeled so much of what God's king was meant to be and to represent, as God's people awaited this descendant of David to come and rule on his throne over his everlasting kingdom.

## Jesus Our Intercessor

All the imperfect God-appointed leaders of Israel were to be a shadow of the perfect mediator, intercessor, and shepherd who would reconcile God's people to himself and cry out on their behalf. Jesus Christ came as that long-expected Son of David (2 Samuel 7:12–16). Jesus was identified as the Son of David (Matthew 1:1; Luke 1:32). Jesus was a more faithful King than David. Jesus was better than Moses (Hebrews 3:3). Jesus did what no other leader of God's people could have done: he gave his life for them. In giving his perfect life as a sacrifice, Jesus became not only the perfect mediator of his people but also the one to reconcile his people to God and cry out on their behalf. Jesus is the great and perfect high priest foreshadowed in the old covenant sacrifices—that high priest of a superior covenant with better promises (Hebrews 8:6).

The most vivid picture of Jesus as the intercessor of his people is found in the moving high priestly prayer, as Jesus prays for his disciples just before going to the cross:

> I pray for them. I am not praying for the world, but
> for those you have given me, for they are yours. All I

have is yours, and all you have is mine. And glory has
come to me through them. I will remain in the world no
longer, but they are still in the world, and I am coming
to you. *Holy Father, protect them by the power of your
name*, the name you gave me, so that they may be one
as we are one ...

My prayer is not that you take them out of the world
but that *you protect them from the evil one*. They are not
of the world, even as I am not of it. *Sanctify them by the
truth*; your word is truth. As you sent me into the world,
I have sent them into the world. For them I sanctify
myself, that they too may be truly sanctified.

**John 17:9 – 11, 15 – 19, italics added**

This impactful prayer during Jesus' anguish of anticipating
the cross reveals so much about the relationship Jesus has with
his Father. Jesus is able to appeal to his Father on behalf of his
disciples in a way no one else could. Jesus came to God as his Son,
equal with God. Jesus asks for their protection. Jesus appeals to
the Father to protect them from the evil one and to sanctify them
in God's truth.

Unlike the intercessors of the past, Jesus comes to the Father
as an equal, and these requests of Jesus are based on who he is,
what he has done, and what he is about to do. When Jesus died on
the cross and rose from the grave, he purchased his people with his
own blood. Now, he is able not just to be the one to deliver God's
message to his people and the people's response to God, but Jesus'
person and work provide unhindered, eternal access to the Father
for his people. This is how Jesus is the Savior of his people, as well
as the perfect mediator and intercessor of his people, as explained
by the author of Hebrews:

But when Christ came as high priest of the good
things that are now already here, he went through the
greater and more perfect tabernacle that is not made
with human hands, that is to say, is not a part of this

creation. He did not enter by means of the blood of goats and calves; but he entered the Most Holy Place once for all by his own blood, thus obtaining eternal redemption. The blood of goats and bulls and the ashes of a heifer sprinkled on those who are ceremonially unclean sanctify them so that they are outwardly clean. How much more, then, will the blood of Christ, who through the eternal Spirit offered himself unblemished to God, cleanse our consciences from acts that lead to death, so that we may serve the living God!

For this reason Christ is the mediator of a new covenant, that those who are called may receive the promised eternal inheritance — now that he has died as a ransom to set them free from the sins committed under the first covenant.          **Hebrews 9:11 – 15**

Because Jesus has now sealed the eternal redemption for every single follower the Father has given him (John 17:6), followers of Jesus can come to the Father with a bold confidence, no longer separated from our Creator:

Therefore, brothers and sisters, since we have confidence to enter the Most Holy Place by the blood of Jesus, by a new and living way opened for us through the curtain, that is, his body, and since we have a great priest over the house of God, let us draw near to God with a sincere heart and with the full assurance that faith brings, having our hearts sprinkled to cleanse us from a guilty conscience and having our bodies washed with pure water.          **Hebrews 10:19 – 22**

Jesus appeals to the Father on his followers' behalf, and they are fully accepted as God's children. Jesus purchased for his followers right standing with his Father that only he is worthy of. God's redemptive plan to reconcile his people is done, once for all, through the sacrifice of Jesus (Hebrews 10:14). As a result, sinners and rebels against God are now adopted as children of God through the atoning sacrifice and righteousness of Jesus Christ. These blood-bought believers in Jesus Christ are now united by Christ in faith, are indwelt by the Holy Spirit, and have become his body—the church.

## The Apostles — Intercessors for the Church

Jesus has brought full reconciliation between God and his redeemed people, and so the church is able to appeal to God on its own through the mediating work of Jesus Christ, who now always lives to make intercession for them (Hebrews 7:25). And yet, as the apostles begin to establish the early church, leaders emerged from among those in the church who lead and shepherd God's people on behalf of the Chief Shepherd (1 Peter 5:4). The apostles modeled this call to a ministry of prayer (Acts 6:4) and then defined this role in their instructions to the different churches. As Paul gives instructions for the church, he also appeals to God, through Christ's mediating work, and models this continuing pattern of God's appointed leaders interceding on behalf of the church:

> Pray in the Spirit on all occasions with all kinds of prayers and requests. With this in mind, be alert and always keep on praying for all the Lord's people. Pray also for me, that whenever I speak, words may be given me so that I will fearlessly make known the mystery of the gospel, for which I am an ambassador in chains. Pray that I may declare it fearlessly, as I should.
>
> **Ephesians 6:18–20**

Paul asks the church members in Ephesus to pray always and on all occasions. To pray for the Lord's people. To pray for Paul and his work of proclaiming the gospel. Paul wrote these words knowing there were faithful pastors (elders) in place (Acts 20:17–38) who would model for their Ephesian flock how to pray in this way (1 Peter 5:3).

James writes to Christians, exhorting them to call on their pastors (elders) to pray on their behalf:

> Is anyone among you in trouble? Let them pray. Is anyone happy? Let them sing songs of praise. Is anyone among you sick? Let them call the elders of the church to pray over them and anoint them with oil in the name of the Lord. And the prayer offered in faith will make the sick person well; the Lord will raise them up. If they have sinned, they will be forgiven. Therefore confess your sins to each other and pray for each other so that you may be healed. The prayer of a righteous person is powerful and effective. **James 5:13–16**

James urges those who are sick to summon their appointed shepherds to pray on their behalf. In these examples, a transition is taking place as the church is being established, one in which the apostles are modeling prayer on behalf of the churches and calling churches to a ministry of prayer as a central aspect of their congregational life—a ministry led by their leaders, their pastors.

## Pastors—Intercessors for Their People

God's redemptive plan and pattern have led to the establishment of the church, where those from every tribe, tongue, people, and nation are transformed through the gospel of Jesus Christ. These redeemed people are brought into a local church led by biblically qualified leaders who shepherd their souls on behalf of the Chief Shepherd, who continually intercedes for them. Those who shepherd on behalf of the Chief Shepherd (1 Peter 5:1–4) and care for the souls of Christ's redeemed people (Hebrews 13:17) are also called to pray for each soul entrusted to their care. An essential aspect of shepherding God's people is praying with them and pleading on their behalf before the Father. The ministry of prayer enables the ministry of God's Spirit and equips the whole body of Christ to obey the commands of Scripture.

This pattern has been a part of God's design to redeem his people from the beginning. God appoints leaders to be intercessors, those who represent the needs of the people to God. Through the work of Christ, every believer now has full access to the throne of God. The prayers of a pastor are not better prayers or necessarily more effective, yet pastors have a special responsibility to diligently make appeals on behalf of their people. Their calling is clear, yet it is all of grace. Praying for the flock is simply one part of the work of being a faithful shepherd.

## Praying for Your Flock

Most pastors would affirm all this. It's not controversial. We know a major aspect of being a faithful shepherd on behalf of the Chief Shepherd is having a regular prayer ministry, praying for the people in our congregations. Yet most of us don't do it. Or if we do, we give minimal time and attention to prayer. I've yet to meet a pastor who feels like he prays too much. Most pastors want to grow in this area, to learn to be more faithful in praying regularly for their people. With this in mind, here are some helpful tools that may help you establish this discipline more faithfully.

### Pray Deliberately

Pastors are shepherds, and Scripture tells us we will give an account for each soul in our care (Hebrews 13:17). Yet we still have a tendency to gravitate to either those we love to be with the most or those who make the most racket and demand our attention. Because of this, some church members unintentionally slip through the cracks.

When I saw this happen in the early years of my ministry, I devised a deliberate system to remind me to pray for my people. It has become an effective and simple way to care for folks and to cut down on unintentional neglect. I created a prayer guide—a booklet with each church member listed in alphabetical order, divided into a twenty-eight day chart. This prayer calendar represents the first twenty-eight days of each month. On day one, I pray for four to five people or family units. After praying for them, I try to make personal contact that day in the form of a home visit, email, handwritten card, phone call, Facebook note, or text message to let them know I prayed for them. In that moment of personal contact, I ask if there is anything I can do to serve them. For those I haven't seen recently, I'll typically make a phone call or schedule a visit with them to get an update on how they are doing in general.

I repeat this process for day two, then day three, and all the way to day twenty-eight. If I am faithful and consistent in this process (which I never do perfectly), I will have prayed and made contact in one month with all who have been entrusted in my care. On the extra days of the month, I do the same thing with our missionaries and others we have sent out into ministry from our church. This has become such a fruitful system for keeping connected with our members that I've encouraged our other pastors to use it. Over time, we've made a prayer guide for our members as well and encouraged them to begin praying for each other. Several of our members have adopted this model and contact folks on the day they pray for them. We've seen amazing fruit as a result! It's wonderful to see members taking prayer seriously, praying for one another's needs, and embracing the priesthood of all believers (1 Peter 2:9).

At one of our women's retreats, a dear woman in the church led a project to take our chart and transfer it to index cards that can sit on a table in the form of a flip calendar. Each morning, a flip of a card shows a list of members who will be prayed for that day. We've done the same in our home, and now our children make a diligent effort to pray for each day's assigned names. They even fight over who gets to flip the card. I have been grateful for and encouraged by our church's response to pray for each other—and all it took was giving them a simple and deliberate way to accomplish it. We may never know until we are with the Lord all the blessings that have come from this prayer guide. It has created a system of accountability for me and the rest of the pastors, helping us to make sure we are deliberately praying for every soul in our flock.

Some pastors have heard me share this and have asked, "Can you do this in a large church?" I admit it can't be done by a single staff member. In a large church, others must shepherd and pray as well. However, after serving on staff at two different churches, each with over 1,500 members, I am convinced each member can still be cared for, known, and prayed for individually by the pastors and leaders. It is possible to have some form of contact for each member each month; it just takes wisdom and creative thinking. The twenty-eight-day chart can be used with a ratio of 1 to 100 in larger settings. In other words, one pastor/elder/staff is assigned to every one hundred members of the church. This breaks down to less than five people or families a day that need to be prayed for and contacted. A five-hundred-member church only needs five shepherds who are willing to put in about thirty minutes a day to accomplish this. A twelve-hundred-member church needs twelve shepherds to pray and contact every member of the church.

Remember, you can't simply stumble into this kind of deliberate effort, regardless of how small or large the church. In fact, you may need to reconfigure the way your staff is set up and operates to make this work. But if you will make the commitment to shepherd and pray for every member of the church, I guarantee that your joy will increase and your people will feel more faithfully cared for by their pastors (Hebrews 13:17).

## Pray with Others

I know from personal experience that the soft voice beckoning pastors to pray for their flocks grows louder when others are involved and you are accountable to them. I gladly admit I would falter in this task even more, allowing other demanding tasks of my ministry to squeeze out prayer, if I didn't have the accountability of other pastors. I recommend you schedule monthly, even weekly times to gather with other pastors, deacons, or other church leaders to pray for the flock. Set aside times to gather solely to pray for the needs of people—no other agendas, just prayer. You can start with a simple twenty- to thirty-minute time early in the morning before work or school. Pick a time, and call your leaders and church to make it a priority. You will learn quickly who is really burdened to gather with others to pray.

Another important way to facilitate praying for the flock with others is to use the meetings you already have scheduled. Carve out the first ten to fifteen minutes of the meeting for prayer. Pastors' meetings, deacons' meetings, small groups, pastoral interns' meetings, staff meetings, and committee meetings are great opportunities to seize. Do more than just offer an opening prayer of a few minutes in length. Involve others, pray for specific needs, and dedicate a significant amount of time for interceding for the church.

At our church, the pastors gather for a four-hour pastors' meeting once a month on Sunday afternoons. We use half of the time to go through the prayer guide mentioned above and pray for every person on the list. There are always church issues that need to be discussed, and it has been tempting to use some of this precious meeting time for business discussions. But I am grateful for the accountability of our other pastors who won't allow me to squeeze out that time. They share the same burden I have to devote a consistent time to pray for our flock.

## Pray Publicly

Most Christian churches reserve a time for prayer in their public gatherings. Yet, sadly, many of these "public" prayers are either general and generic or focus on needs outside the local church. At other times, public prayers become nothing more than a list of never-ending requests that often have to do with superficial needs. Public worship is probably not the time to pray for the recovery of Aunt Millie's dog—especially when Aunt Millie isn't even a member of the church! When pastors neglect to pray for the real and pressing needs of church members during a weekly public gathering, they miss a huge opportunity to model for members the way the church should pray for one another.

A pastoral prayer in the service is a great time to pray for these specific needs. This is a time to pray for *specific* people in the church, especially those who are sick and suffering. Appropriate issues include recent marriages, parenting-related challenges, battles with sin, growth in discipleship, evangelistic opportunities, wisdom for church leaders, and blessing and empowerment for those who are heading out to engage in ministry or mission work. Praying for these needs publicly also informs the congregation about what is happening in the life of the church. It allows pastors to model how the congregation should spiritually understand these issues and how they, too, can pray for these needs. These specific, meaningful prayer concerns should be chosen wisely and carefully, and you may need to first seek permission in certain circumstances. And these are by no means the only topics to cover in a public worship service. Whatever is prayed for publicly is highlighted as something important and valuable, and in the long term it can lead to a congregational prayer ministry for the entire congregation.

It is also beneficial for pastors to pray for evangelistic efforts in the community (Colossians 4:3), for other local churches (Ephesians 1:15–16), and for mission efforts that are supported by the church (1 Corinthians 16:9). In addition to lifting up the needs of the community and the mission of the church, this informs church members and models for them how to pray for others. It can also remind them of ways the Lord might want to use them to take the gospel to others. These public prayers can motivate your flock to engage in kingdom work as salt and light in the world. A pastor who prays for these things will strengthen the hands of his people as they go out into the world to minister to others.

## Conclusion

Christian pastors have been given a great gift, namely, the ability to intercede for the needs of their flock through the mediatorial work of Jesus and the presence of the Holy Spirit. As pastors, we are not called to be the intercessor and mediator who reconciles our people to God. That work has already been fully and completely accomplished in the life, death, and resurrection of Jesus Christ. Jesus now reigns at the right hand of God, interceding for all who have trusted in Christ and been transformed by the gospel. Our calling is to be stewards of this intercession. As part of our work as shepherds, as pastors, we bring the needs of God's people to the Chief Shepherd. What better way for us to shepherd God's people than to go to our Father and plead for them in the name of Jesus?

Respond to the soft voice in your heart that beckons you to pray. Make it a priority to respond and to create daily disciplines that systematically enable you to pray for all of your people. Involve others in this work, and rejoice together that you have full access to God because of the perfect mediating work of our Redeemer.

part 2
# focus

## Chapter 4

# Set an Example

> Don't let anyone look down on you because you are
> young, but set an example for the believers in speech,
> in conduct, in love, in faith and in purity.
>
> **1 Timothy 4:12**

Having served on staff at several churches, I've seen a variety of different models of pastoral leadership over the years. In one church, the pastor functioned much like a CEO. He never visited the sick or the widows. He didn't write his own sermons but had two full-time research assistants do this for him each week. Unfortunately, he had zero accountability with other leaders. I immediately knew he was not an example for me to imitate. Others on staff were enamored with his leadership and aspired to be like him. They believed he had reached the pinnacle of success as a pastor, and they wanted what he had.

Thankfully, a pastor from another church began to invest in me from afar. He met with me and taught me from the Bible what a pastor is and what he is supposed to do. He taught me what the Bible says about the local church and how to pursue genuine health within the church. He taught me that God has a design for his shepherds and his church. He also reminded me of my need to pay close attention to my own life. For several years, I was living in a paradox. Working at my church, I'd see a clear example of pastoral leadership, yet not one I could admire. At the same time, from afar I'd learn about a radically different model of pastoral identity and leadership. I realized I was at a crossroads. The choices I made at that moment would determine my future calling.

The examples we place before us can have a massive influence on the way we think and live. Whether they are good or bad examples, they shape us into who we become. It's true for parents as they raise their children, for bosses in the way they treat their employees, and for leaders and pastors in the church, those called to shepherd God's people. This is one of the reasons that Paul urged his young protégés in the ministry, Titus and Timothy, to grasp how essential it was to set examples for other pastors to follow. Paul also urged them to be examples for their flocks. And the same is true for us. Every pastor is an example — good or bad — to other pastors and to his own flock. What are you modeling to others? What kind of example are you?

## Pastors, Set an Example

The godly, faithful life of pastors, or the lack thereof, will set the tone for the entire church they serve. This is one of the reasons Paul outlines clear and specific characteristics that every pastor must possess to even qualify for the office (1 Timothy 3:1 – 7). But Paul is not the only voice that speaks to this need in the New Testament; other apostles highlight this as well and urge pastors to set an example for others.

### Model a Godly Example

Paul urges Timothy, a young and inexperienced pastor, to be an example to other believers, highlighting specific areas of focus: "Don't let anyone look down on you because you are young, but set an example for the believers in speech, in conduct, in love, in faith and in purity" (1 Timothy 4:12).

As Paul's life and ministry were coming to a close, he wasn't concerned about age or experience. If anything, Timothy's youth made it even more important to stress that he be sure to "set an example for the believers." Paul knew that sheep look to their shepherd. It doesn't matter whether or not that shepherd is a faithful, godly example; either way he will have a deep impact on his sheep.

Paul gives some details in areas of character that should give evidence of gospel transformation. Timothy is to be an example in speech, conduct, love, faith, and purity. Paul is calling Timothy to be an example to others in what he says, in how he acts, and in what spiritual realities motivate his speech and action.

## Be a Humble Example

The apostle Peter also reminds pastors they are an example to others. In a flurry of words to his fellow shepherds, Peter highlights the importance of being an example that others should follow:

> Be shepherds of God's flock that is under your care, watching over them — not because you must, but because you are willing, as God wants you to be; not pursuing dishonest gain, but eager to serve; not lording it over those entrusted to you, but being examples to the flock. **1 Peter 5:2-3**

Peter brings to light the need for a pastor to be an example of *humble and honest service*. He shows what a good example looks like by contrasting it with several bad examples of leadership. There are pastors who sincerely desire to care for Christ's flock, yet sadly there are also pastors who operate under an obligatory, dishonest, self-serving narcissism, much as I experienced in my early years of church ministry. The honest truth is that no pastor is a completely faithful example. Every pastor is in constant need of the cleansing blood of Christ. Yet this does not absolve pastors of responsibility for how they act. Paul and Peter are both clear: A pastor's sanctification should set the pace for others' pursuits of holiness.

### Remember Good Examples

In Hebrews 13, the author exhorts his audience to walk in several different ways that will demonstrate they are persevering in their faith in Jesus. He sums up a list of exhortations with these sobering words for leaders: "Remember your leaders, who spoke the word of God to you. Consider the outcome of their way of life and imitate their faith" (Hebrews 13:7).

I'll never forget a late-night conversation with one of my pastoral mentors. I was nearing the conclusion of the interview process with the church where I would become the senior pastor, and they had invited me to preach. My mentor asked me a series of thoughtful questions, and then there was a moment when he summarized it all with a word of blessing: "Well, I have affirmed your gifts. I have taught you everything I know. Go to pastor that church, and know I will be praying for you."

These were simple words, but there was so much enfolded in what he said to me that day. The unspoken message behind everything he said was, *I have taught and invested in you, and I am counting on you, with God's help, to be faithful and a good steward of what you have been taught.* I regularly think about that time and recall those words. They encourage me and inspire me to be faithful as a leader and as a follower of Christ. We must never forget that we as pastors are where we are today because someone first spoke the word of God to us, taught us, and invested in us. Now we are in the privileged position as preachers of God's word and pastors of God's people to do the same in the lives of others.

The leaders that the writer of Hebrews is speaking of spoke the word of God with their words and deeds. One reason the writer is so adamant that they remember the example of their leaders is that the holy conduct and persevering faith these leaders modeled affirm the truth of the gospel they preach. This strongly implies that if these believers reject their faith in Christ, they will be rejecting those who led them well, faithfully spoke God's word to them, and powerfully lived it out before them. The message and the messenger are closely linked.

Set an Example

These passages also imply a *personal* relationship — that the pastor knows the people he is mentoring. A common trend today, especially among younger pastors, is to idolize popular, well-known pastors as a substitute for one-on-one mentoring. Pastors listen to their sermons, read their books, and hear them speak at conferences. And while the influence of these popular pastors can be good and helpful in many ways, it should not replace interaction with a flesh-and-blood pastoral mentor who knows our life and ministry and can speak into it. Every pastor needs someone they can be honest with, an example they can follow.

## You Are Now the Example!

Consider once again this exhortation: "Remember your leaders, who spoke the word of God to you. Consider the outcome of their way of life and imitate their faith" (Hebrews 13:7).

Pastors are indebted to those who taught them, invested in them, and helped guide them to where they are today in their life and ministry. Pastors honor the investment their mentors have made into their lives as they faithfully press on to shepherd others. At the same time, we must recognize that none of this can be done in our own power. Living a godly, faithful life is the result of the grace of God working through the transforming power of the gospel. Great gifts and abilities will not always lead to a godly example. Only the power of the gospel at work on the heart of a pastor will accomplish this work. Only the gospel, daily applied to our lives, can make us be the model our people need to see.

Though we must acknowledge that living a godly life and being a faithful example for others come only through the power of Christ at work in each of us, I can think of several practical ways to grow as an example to others. Some of these require persistence over time; others necessitate a reordering of priorities. Yet I trust you will see the long-term benefits.

## *Honor Your Ministry Heroes*

It is helpful for pastors to recall the impact of the people who invested in them, spoke God's word to them, and taught them about ministry. I remember receiving a phone call early one cold November morning with the sad news that my dear friend and pastoral mentor, Jackson, had been killed in a head-on collision with a drunk driver. Jackson and I had a very special friendship. Jackson planted Dayspring Fellowship Church and pastored there more than thirty years. He was a model of faithfulness, endurance, and steadfast love to that flock. I always told others that Jackson was the man I wanted to be when I grew up. He set the bar for me as a model of the kind of pastor I want to be.

My last conversation with Jackson took place about a month before he died. I was on my way to conduct the funeral of a dear woman in our church who was three months shy of turning 107. I called Jackson to say hello and just to hear his voice again. Typically I would call for counsel and advice, but this time, for some reason, I felt led to call him and see how he was doing and to thank him for being my friend and mentor.

I said to him, "Jackson, I have no difficult situation to mention to you, no advice to seek. I just wanted to see how you were doing and how Barbara's recovery from surgery was going. I also just wanted to say how grateful I am for you and all you have done to teach and invest in me. You have impacted me as a man, husband, father, and pastor more than you will ever know. You and your pastoral example are a gift from God. Thank you for your friendship and all you have done!"

Looking back, I see the kindness of God in leading me to make that call. Our sovereign and good God, who numbers our days before we live a single one (Psalm 139:16), knew what I did not know: this was my last conversation with Jackson this side of eternity. Thinking about this conversation and the events that followed is a great motivator to continually remember the others who set an example for me and to regularly take time to honor them. It's not hard to give them a call or send an email and say thank you. I encourage you to do this today to whomever is on your mind right now. You won't regret it!

The letter to the Hebrews urges us to *remember* those who led us, those who spoke the word of God to us. As you remember, contact them soon, honor them in some way, and thank God for placing this person—a faithful parent, pastor, teacher, or friend—as an extension of his sovereign care for you. These men and women were placed in your life to help you persevere in your faith in Jesus. God used them to bring you to where you are today and to prepare you for the ministry to which you have been called. Remember them and give thanks.

## Spend Time with Your People

We cannot set an example for others if we do not spend time with them. More and more, I hear from young pastors who are adopting a ministry model in which they spend forty hours a week in their study, delegating things like visitation and discipleship to their deacons and other leaders in the church. I see many problems with this approach to pastoral ministry, but an obvious one is the lack of time spent with people in the church. How can a pastor set an example for his people if he only sees them once a week? A pastor should certainly prepare to preach the word, but the word must be ministered both publicly and privately. A pastor best accomplishes this by going to where his people are and spending time with them. Where are your people during the week? You may want to meet with a young professional at his workplace, visit an elderly woman in her home and work in her garden with her, or invite a young married couple to your home to talk about the challenges and joys of marriage and raising a family. Let them see the example of your own family life as they set out to establish theirs. The shepherd must spend time with the sheep if he wants to be the example God calls him to be.

### Stop Making Excuses

Early in my ministry training, I was taught to make excuses when I couldn't get my work done. At the young age of twenty, I served in my first staff position, and my ministry supervisor said to me, "Look, you are young, so no one is going to take you seriously. Just do the best you can, and one day you might be respected and heard and actually have an impact on people." Yet those words run counter to the wisdom of the apostle Paul, who encouraged young Timothy: "Don't let anyone look down on you because you are young, but set an example for the believers in speech, in conduct, in love, in faith and in purity" (1 Timothy 4:12). Paul tells Timothy to set an example—and also to stand up against the low expectations of others. If you run into challenges and difficulties in ministry, if people don't listen to you or take you seriously, don't have a pity party. Seek to overcome the obstacles. In my early years, I could have easily used the words of my supervisor as a license to coast through my work, to take the easy path.

Being young is just one excuse I've heard pastors make. We all have a tendency to cop out of our responsibility to set an example before our family and flock. We may not actually say, "Do as I say, not as I do," but if we are not careful to watch ourselves, our lives begin to communicate this sinful attitude. Excuses turn us into victims and absolve us of responsibility. They tempt us to stop battling against our sin as we should. Excuses can even make us critical of others, propelling us to blame them for our failures or disappointments. We begin to lower the biblical standard set before us. Pastors are certainly not immune; we are prone to make excuses, just like everyone else.

Don't excuse yourself from your biblical calling to set an example for the flock. Yes, you are a sinner, and you are not perfect. God knows that pastors need the cleansing blood of Jesus and the good news of what Jesus has done, just as much as anyone else. But we also know that God sets a higher standard for leaders. Our acceptance before God has already been fully met for us in Christ. So seek to be an example to others in *freedom*, knowing Christ has already met the standard you could never meet. You are now clothed in Jesus' righteousness. Walk humbly in that righteousness, acknowledging your sin and weaknesses as a leader and setting a hope-filled example for your people. The chief example we set for our people is to show them that we as pastors live and breathe the gospel ourselves.

## Acknowledge Your Weakness

Walking in the truth of the gospel will require the humility to admit when we are wrong and to acknowledge our mistakes and our sins against others. Paul outlines several clear characteristics that should be evident in a pastor's life (1 Timothy 3:1–7). And while being kind, loving, and gracious to others is one way to set an example, a pastor also models the gospel through his humble transparency when he fails to exemplify these characteristics. Arguably, the best example a pastor can set for his family and flock is through brokenness and authenticity. I say this because it is often one of the hardest things to do as a pastor and a leader. It's not easy to share a self-incriminating story or to give a negative example about yourself in a sermon, and certainly wisdom is needed when you share details. At the same time, I've discovered that when I provide an honest glimpse of my own failings, my people are able to connect with me in a unique and special way. Folks I haven't heard from for a while come up and want to talk. Others want to meet later in the week for prayer and counsel. Weakness is more winsome than we realize.

Your people will naturally place you on a pedestal and treat you as a "special" Christian, above the average, until you willingly and boldly knock down this reverential treatment in front of your flock. When you do this and show them you struggle with sin, just as they do, your people will begin to connect with you in a special way. They will come to understand that their pastor is just as weak, broken, and in need of God's grace as they are. Setting an example for your family and flock does not mean doing everything right and never making a mistake. Your church and your family know you are a sinner, even if you never acknowledge it. You don't do everything right at all times. Accept this, acknowledge it, and model a humble, transparent brokenness before your people to set an example of what it looks like to walk in the grace of God. Depend on God's grace, and show others how to rest in the mercy of God in Christ.

## Encourage Your People to Imitate You

Of all the guidance I've shared so far in this chapter, this tidbit may well be the most difficult for pastors today. Again, recall that the writer of Hebrews exhorts Christians to look to their leaders and "consider the outcome of their way of life and imitate their faith" (Hebrews 13:7). Pastors should be so aware of their own sins, struggles, and weaknesses that they tremble at the thought of ever saying to their people, "Do what I do. Say what I say. Imitate my faith." And yet that is exactly what the Bible calls pastors to do. Pastors should not just speak God's word; they should also model it in such a way that they can honestly say to others, "Follow me." As a pastor boldly speaks God's word, he should passionately live out what he speaks so that others will follow.

I once had the privilege of hearing Pastor Al Martin speak to a group of pastors, and he said something that deeply affected me. He was talking about being an example for the flock: "What does your church member do when a non-Christian walks through the door and asks them how a Christian man should treat his wife? You know what they should do? They should point to you, their pastor, and say, "Watch him. He's my pastor. You need to watch the way he tenderly, lovingly, and sacrificially cherishes that woman next to him."

This is our charge as pastors—that by the grace of God we can shepherd our people as sinners who have been changed by the gospel and called out by the Chief Shepherd. We are not perfect in doing this, but we can be faithful.

## Conclusion

Jackson Boyett, the dear friend and mentor I mentioned earlier, had two men he trained, discipled, and invested in who eventually went to a local seminary. These men later became a part of our church. After many years of faithful service in our church, one of them took an associate pastor position at another church and the other was sent out to be Jackson's successor at Dayspring. A month before they departed, I had the opportunity to have lunch with them and tell them what a joy it had been to serve with them and to invest in their lives. I urged them to carry on the work that Jackson had started and passed to me. I told them that since Jackson wasn't there to give them a parting charge, I would do it on his behalf. I read Hebrews 13:7 and said, "As you now go to shepherd God's people in your own flock, remember those who led you, who spoke the word of God to you; and as you consider the result of their conduct, imitate their faith."

You have an extraordinary honor. Not only are you the beneficiary of the example of others—of those who faithfully led you, spoke God's word to you, and powerfully lived that word with you—you now have the opportunity to do the same with those under your care. Every pastor is charged to set an example, one that has been modeled for them. May the weight of this encourage you as you grab hold of the good news of the gospel, not crushing you with expectations you can never meet but spurring you on to steadfast and faithful ministry as you model how to run to the cross when you fail to be a perfect example to others.

Chapter 5

# Visit the Sick

"I needed clothes and you clothed me, I was sick and
you looked after me, I was in prison and you came to
visit me."                                    **Matthew 25:36**

One of the essential aspects of pastoral ministry is becoming increasingly obsolete today.* I find that many pastors
are ignoring or neglecting their responsibility to care for those in
their flock who are suffering through sickness, pain, disease, and
other forms of physical infirmities. For centuries, the ministry of a
pastor was marked by individual soul care in the key, providential
moments of people's lives. And suffering brought on by sickness
is one of those times. Today, some in the younger generation of
pastors prefer to specialize in a particular ministry like preaching
or leadership and leave the care of the sick to others. I don't believe
this form of specialization is good or biblical, and in this chapter
I hope to convince the busiest of pastors that caring for the sick is
still a top priority for pastoral ministry.

## The Biblical Call to the Sick

Biblically, it's clear that God calls pastors to care for the sick
and afflicted. This isn't just rooted in a couple of key passages; it
is woven throughout the whole of Scripture and is highlighted by

---

*This chapter summarizes content originally published in Brian Croft, *Visit
the Sick* (Grand Rapids: Zondervan, 2014).

two themes: (1) God is sovereign over sickness and healing, and (2) God calls his people to care for the needy and afflicted.

## Creation and Fall

The Bible begins its historical narrative with a world that is foreign to us today. God created the heavens, the earth, and all the living creatures (Genesis 1–2). He also created man and woman in his image (1:27) and saw that all he had made was very good (1:31). He placed the man and woman in the garden of Eden, where they were to rule over his creation and be fruitful and increase in number. In this world there was also the absence of sickness, pain, disease, suffering, and affliction. No cancer preyed on human bodies. No aches and pains plagued the body. No disease needed to be healed, nor did any sickness need to be cured. Most significantly, there was no death. All was good, perfect, and right, as God intended for his creation.

Nevertheless, the world of Genesis 1–2 is not the world we live in today. The reality of life today is that something is really wrong with the world and with those who are made in God's image. According to Genesis 3, Adam and Eve sinned by disobeying God's word in eating from the tree of the knowledge of good and evil (verse 6). As a result, the curse of death came on them and all of his creation, just as God had warned. On that day, sin with all of its ramifications entered the world. Adam and Eve were removed from the garden and the tree of life, whose fruit would grant eternal life (verse 22). As a result, man would not just suffer death, but also the effects of death, such as old age, pain, and suffering.

Sickness and disease are part of the curse resulting from sin. We have many explanations today about what sickness is and how it came to exist. The Bible, however, simplifies a complicated topic. Sickness, disease, pain, suffering, affliction, and death are undeniable evidences of the fall of mankind. From this place in the story line of the Bible, the desperate need for redemption begins. It is quickly revealed in this narrative that only a sovereign, eternal

God can intervene to save creation from this curse. Therefore, the hope of the gospel, which includes the promise of physical resurrection, begins to unfold in a glorious work of redemption that will culminate in Jesus' death and resurrection.

## The Life of Israel

God decided to redeem mankind through a chosen nation that would be his people among all the other nations of the earth. This nation was promised to Abraham (Genesis 12) through a child, Isaac, who was yet to be born (Genesis 21). From this child, the nation of Israel (the descendants of Jacob, Isaac's child) would begin. Through Isaac's grandson Joseph the nation of Israel was established in Egypt, where they multiplied greatly (Exodus 1:7), yet eventually became enslaved to the Egyptians. However, hundreds of years before this bondage, God promised he would deliver them from their oppression and judge the nation that held them captive (Genesis 15:13–14). Through the events of this deliverance, God would use sickness and disease for his purposes and glory. This is seen in the judgments against Pharaoh (Exodus 9; 11) and in God's protection of Israel (Exodus 15:26). This theme is highlighted in the promise of the old covenant, in which God promised blessings for obedience and curses for disobedience (Deuteronomy 28–29).

The evidence of God's purposes in sickness and disease continues in both judgment and healing as Israel enters the Promised Land and human kings begin to rule over them. God causes King David's son to become sick and die because of David's adultery (2 Samuel 12:14–18). King Asa becomes diseased in his feet. Though his disease is severe, he seeks help from physicians instead of the Lord and dies (2 Chronicles 16:12–13). Yet God's powerful hand brings healing to King Hezekiah, who is mortally ill and has been told he will die (2 Kings 20:1–11). God brings healing to a little boy through Elijah as a result of the mother's plea to the

Lord (1 Kings 17:17–24). In the midst of judgment on disobedience, God also shows his kindness.

God's unfolding story line to redeem also reveals the call to his people to care for those who suffer the affliction of sickness and disease. God, through the prophet Ezekiel, chastises the shepherds of Israel for neglecting their flock, which they do in several ways, including failing to care for the sick. Ezekiel writes, "You have not strengthened the weak or healed the sick or bound up the injured. You have not brought back the strays or searched for the lost. You have ruled them harshly and brutally" (Ezekiel 34:4). The shepherds' neglect in caring for the sick will naturally lead other people to neglect them too.

Throughout Israel's history, God uses sickness, disease, and affliction as a divine design to achieve his purposes. The prophets conclude that God's people are scattered, disobedient, and discouraged; yet the prophets encourage them to wait for the hope of the promised redeemer and healer. Despite this tragic history of God's people, God is faithful to the covenant he made with his people to send a redeemer and usher in the long-awaited kingdom of God.

## The Life of Christ

After many years of silence, God breaks through the despair and suffering with a voice calling in the wilderness to prepare the way for the Lord (Mark 1:3). Mark displays, all throughout his account, the evidence that Jesus came in the authority of God as the Son of God (Mark 1:1), and a primary evidence of this coming kingdom in him is his authority over sickness, disease, and death. All the gospel writers remind the reader of this reality in a constant pattern of summary: "News about [Jesus] spread all over Syria, and people brought to him all who were ill with various diseases, those suffering severe pain, the demon-possessed, those having seizures, and the paralyzed; and he healed them" (Matthew 4:24). Jesus healed many and thus fulfilled the prophets' words.

This evidence of Jesus' authority and the coming kingdom is most clearly seen in Jesus' raising of the dead. Jesus revives the synagogue leader's little girl who had died (Mark 5:41–42). He raises Lazarus from the dead after days of being in the tomb (John 11:43–44). Ultimately, Jesus' raising of the dead was to point to his own physical resurrection three days after dying on the cross. In the Messiah's own resurrection, his followers are not only promised eternal life through repentance and faith in him; they are promised a physical resurrection on the final day: "If we have been united with him in a death like his, we will certainly also be united with him in a resurrection like his" (Romans 6:5). In this resurrection, his followers have the promise of being citizens of the eternal kingdom of God.

God's sovereign power over sickness and disease in Jesus' authority is undeniable throughout the gospel accounts. Equally present is the call Jesus gives to his followers to care for those who are afflicted. The clearest example is in Matthew 25, where Jesus teaches his disciples a parable about kingdom living in caring for others in his name: "I was hungry and you gave me something to eat, I was thirsty and you gave me something to drink, I was a stranger and you invited me in, I needed clothes and you clothed me, I was sick and you looked after me, I was in prison and you came to visit me" (verses 35–36). Jesus powerfully teaches that the king's subjects cared for him in those moments when they cared for one of the least of these brothers (verse 40). He ends this teaching with a word about the judgment that falls on the wicked who did not care for him as evidenced by their neglect to care for others (verses 41–46).

Jesus ushers in the kingdom of God, and a primary evidence that redemption has come is that the blind see, the lame walk, the deaf hear, the sick and diseased are healed, and the dead are raised. God has designed his people to care for one another as a powerful representation of his compassion for the weak and needy. As the narrative continues to unfold, these glorious evidences of the kingdom of God are further seen in the birth and life of Christ's church.

### The Life of the Church

When Jesus sent out his disciples, he commanded them to "heal the sick, raise the dead, cleanse those who have leprosy, drive out demons" (Matthew 10:8). These commands come to fulfillment as the church is empowered at Pentecost (Acts 2) and as the apostles go out to be Christ's witnesses to the world (Acts 1:8). Through the apostles we find demonstrations of God's sovereign power to judge, as well as to heal, according to his purposes. Ananias and Sapphira receive divine judgment in death because they lied about giving the full portion of the proceeds from their sold property to the apostles (Acts 5:1–11). God also heals as a measure of compassion on Tabitha and those who loved her; as she fell sick and died, Peter raises her from the dead (Acts 9:36–43).

In the letters, God's sovereign redemptive purposes in sickness and suffering are seen. Paul was given a thorn in his flesh so that the power of Christ would be most powerfully displayed in his weakness (2 Corinthians 12:8–9). Sickness and death were used as means to warn the church against abusing the Lord's Table (1 Corinthians 11:27–30). Peter urged Christians who suffer according to the will of God to see this as a time to entrust their souls to their faithful Creator (1 Peter 4:19). The sovereign God of the universe has used sickness, pain, disease, and suffering as a way to sanctify his kingdom people and magnify the worth of Christ.

There is also the call on those in the church to care sacrificially for the afflicted in order to achieve these redemptive purposes. A powerful example of this calling comes in the book of Acts when Christians sell their properties and lay the proceeds at the apostles' feet to be used to serve those in need (Acts 4:34–37). Paul refers to Epaphroditus's sickness as he writes to the church in Philippi, and there is evident care and concern from both Paul and the church in this matter (Philippians 2:25–27). James exhorts Christians to call on the elders to pray for the sick (James 5:14). John prays that Christians "may enjoy good health and that all may go well" with them (3 John 2). In these examples, Christians show sympathy for the sick and needy. The call of sacrificial action to one another exists for the Christian. A trust in God's sovereign design to be accomplished in sickness is necessary. There is a call on the individual Christian and the local church body to care for those in the church who are sick, hurting, afflicted, and suffering until Jesus returns for his church and consummates his kingdom.

## New Creation

One day, the unfolding of God's redemptive plan for all creation will come to an end. The final destination for those who follow Christ is not a disembodied existence of life after death. When Jesus returns, he will come for his bride, judge the nations, punish the wicked, and fully consummate his kingdom in the new heaven and the new earth. This state is known as the new creation, where the curse of sin is fully and permanently reversed. There God's kingdom people will experience not just physical resurrection but eternal fellowship with Jesus our Savior and King.

A wonderful hope in this coming promise is that we will have physically whole bodies that are not cursed. In other words, there will be no more sickness, disease, pain, suffering, affliction, and death (Revelation 20:14). John gives a vivid picture in the book of Revelation: "He will wipe every tear from their eyes. There will be no more death or mourning or crying or pain" (21:4). In a vision reminiscent of Eden (Genesis 2), John also speaks of a centrally located river and tree of life whose leaves are for the healing of the nations (Revelation 22:1–2). The curse has been reversed, and those who belong to the kingdom of God through the cross of Christ will experience what God intended in the garden of Eden.

Understanding this unfolding story line of the Bible is essential not only to grasp God's design and plan for his creation, but to comprehend God's eternal purpose in the reality of sickness, disease, pain, and affliction in the world. As pastors seek to visit and care for the sick and afflicted in our congregations, it is essential we not just remember God's plan in sickness, but we confess that a sovereign God rules over it all and is at work for the good of his people (Romans 8:28). This biblical reality will inform us as we seek to minister grace and will empower us to consider how best to care for those we visit.

## What to Do When Visiting the Sick

The Scriptures are undeniably clear about the purposes of a sovereign God throughout redemptive history to use sickness, disease, and affliction in the lives of his people to achieve his redemptive purposes for his own glory. The Bible is, however, not as clear on how to flesh out these biblical principles in the everyday life of our specific context. Here are a few practical tools for pastors and others to use in their effort to put these biblical imperatives into practice in ways that are both helpful and effective as they care for the sick in their congregations.

### Ask Questions

We must be deliberate about our conversations when visiting the sick. If we are going to be faithful in this task, then we need to anticipate leading these interactions. The best way to prepare is to consider what kinds of questions will eventually lead to spiritual conversation. However, as we prepare, we must remember those to whom we are talking. They are, at the very least, uncomfortable because of the circumstances. Yet they may also be dealing with intense pain, be in and out of consciousness, or be distracted by family members in the room. Therefore, before we begin to ask questions, we should heed the wise counsel of David Dickson: "Don't let us strain them with anything requiring long or continuous attention, and let our change from one subject to another be natural and easy."[10]

It is only after we've given thoughtful consideration about what we should ask that we should proceed. Here is a progression that has proven helpful for me. Ask the sick about themselves, their condition, and the kind of recommended treatment. Ask about their family, specifically in regard to who has been caring for them during this time. Then try to turn the conversation to one of a spiritual nature. A helpful way to do this is to ask how you can pray for them. The Holy Spirit often will open up opportunities through this question to talk about eternal issues. However, our questions are meant to lead us to talk about God and the hope found only in Christ. This is our hope, whether a person is sick or healthy. Therefore, our questions should be sensitive to patients' circumstances but always God honoring and gospel driven in content.

### Read Scripture

A young seminary student in my church decided to visit a dying member in the hospital. Though he had very little experience, he had heard me challenge the congregation to care for this longtime, faithful member during a sudden turn for the worse. He walked into her hospital room to find the woman in a most disturbing state. She was semiconscious, gasping for every breath and having seizures. He also stumbled onto a highly unusual occurrence—no family in the room. He had heard me say, "There is always family in the room to talk to." This time, however, there were no family members. What would you have done? This faithful brother had an impactful and spiritually mature response.

He opened his Bible and began to read. As he stood next to the bed of this dying woman who was gasping for breath, he read about the glorious character of God and his faithful promises to his adopted children in Christ. She died soon after this faithful brother left the room. Only God knows the fruit of that afternoon. But we need to see how sound his instincts were in that moment. It is God's word that is "alive and active" and "sharper than any double-edged sword" (Hebrews 4:12). We must have the truth of God's word on our lips; otherwise, we may not respond well when faced with such uncomfortable moments. Thomas Murphy, a faithful nineteenth-century American pastor, urges pastors to make the reading of Scripture a central priority in their visit:

> Even when patients are very weak, we should read the word, quote it, repeat so as to impress it, emphasize and explain its rich instructions. Through many examples given by Dr. Archibald Alexander and others, it has been proved that the simple teachings of God's book, presented to the minds of even skeptical and doubting patients, is often far better than any process of argument that can be entered into with them. To read or quote passages of Scripture will frequently be a great relief to the pastor when the case is so serious and pressing that, of himself, he is utterly at a loss what to say. Indeed, this is often almost all that can be done, when the patient either cannot or will not speak, and when we are scarcely sure that any words are heard. It is well, therefore, for ministers to have a large store of passages suitable for the sick laid up in memory and ready for use. There should be deliberate and continued preparation for this, as it is a matter which we cannot afford to overlook.[11]

How can we prepare for these types of situations? According to Murphy's counsel, we should have "a large store of passages suitable for the sick laid up in memory and ready for use." Take the time to think through several Scriptures that can be an encouragement to those who are sick. It is helpful to place these in categories. Here are four examples for a variety of situations:

- **Passages of comfort:** Psalms 23; 28; 34; 46; 62; 145; Hebrews 4:14–16
- **Succinct gospel passages:** John 11:25–26; Romans 5:6–11; 2 Corinthians 5:17–21; Ephesians 2:1–10
- **Passages dealing with the purpose of suffering for the believer:** 2 Corinthians 12:7–9; James 1:2–4; 1 Peter 1:6–7; 4:12–19

90

- **Passages related to the reality and hope of eternity with Christ:** John 10:27–30; 14:1–3; Philippians 1:21–23; 1 Peter 1:3–5

Having a few passages in mind will allow you to be better equipped for the unexpected. Just in case you missed the obvious, *bring your Bible*.

## Pray the Gospel

One morning, a nurse at a local hospital called me to request my immediate presence. The non-Christian spouse of one of our members was moments away from dying. I had no idea what awaited me when I arrived. I walked into a room full of family members as the heartbroken husband motioned me over to his wife's bed. He was also suffering from medical problems that resulted in a tracheostomy and prevented him from speaking.

However, it didn't take me long to see why I had been summoned. He was asking me to pray for his wife as the doctor prepared to take her off the ventilator. Twenty minutes before, I had been in my office, neck-deep in my studies; now I was being asked to pray a final prayer over a dying, non-Christian woman in front of her husband and some fifteen non-Christian family members who were hanging on to a miracle with my prayer. I literally had a few seconds to decide what to do and how to pray.

I decided to pray the gospel for this dying woman, her husband, and the non-Christian family members who filled the room. I did not pray that God would spare her. I did not pray that God would heal her. I did not pray some manipulating request that God would receive her (which is what I think they expected me to pray). I prayed that the gospel was her only hope in such a way that God could let every person in that room know it was their only hope also. Praying the gospel does not have to be complicated. It can be something as simple as praying the four main areas of the gospel: *God, Man, Christ, Response.*

God taught an invaluable lesson that day in the hospital room, which has had a profound impact on me and my ministry. When the gospel is prayed, the gospel is heard. When I prayed the gospel in the room that day, it was for this dying woman (moments from facing judgment), her Christian husband, and her lost family members to hear. If we truly believe faith comes from hearing (Romans 10:17), we should never leave a hospital room, nursing home, rehabilitation center, or home of a sick person (or healthy person, for that matter) without praying the hope of God in Christ.

### Leave a Note

When I first started making hospital visits, I often found that my effort was in vain—not because of a bad visit, but because I wasn't able to see the sick person. Often I simply left and came back a few hours later—only to find that I'd still missed seeing them. I was wasting valuable time driving back and forth, and my efforts were being met with discouragement. Unfortunately, no one had shared with me a simple and obvious tactic: *leave a note*.

We encounter a number of different situations in which the people we want to visit will be unavailable. If they are hospitalized, they may be out of the room for tests or procedures, or they may be resting. Doctors or nurses may be in for consultation or treatments, and so our patient is not available for a visit. In a nursing home they may be occupied with recreational activities, or they may be resting and unavailable. Patients in rehab centers often leave their room to do therapy several times a day. Even in situations where we visit someone at their own home, we may find they are out to a medical appointment or resting and unable to receive visitors.

Leaving a note in these kinds of scenarios is a fruitful solution because it accomplishes several aspects of care we would have pursued had we been able to see them. A note lets them know we took the time to seek them out and that we are praying for them. It communicates that we want to serve them in any way we can and that they remain connected to their church despite their circumstances. They can read our note over and over again for encouragement long after we have gone.

Additionally, it can be valuable to leave little books or tracts to keep the patient occupied with the truths you spoke and prayed with them. Thomas Murphy affirms this practice:

> Pages which contain truths just applicable to them will often be perused in their long hours of languishment, and the appropriate instruction found in them will be pondered over and over again. Then the silent message from the printed lines can be received without the excitement or perturbation which the visit of even the minister will often produce. Sometimes the little volume of gospel comfort will be most welcome as a help to cheer the weary hours. If the patient himself is not able to read, generally some Christian friend will be glad to read for him, and so convey the words of life to the hungry soul.[12]

Leaving a note and other appropriate readable resources can serve a patient well when the hours drag on and the flow of visitors slows down.

## Touch with Discernment

The effective use of physical touch is not dependent on whether you are a touchy-feely person. Appropriate physical touch often communicates a love and care that words cannot. Those who are sick can easily develop "leprosy syndrome." In the first century, leprosy caused one to be banished from the city limits and totally ostracized. Imagine what it must have felt like to be treated so badly and to be so unloved, all because of a physical stigma. The sick, especially those in a hospital context, can develop this feeling of ostracism easily. Thus, one of the most effective ways to communicate love to suffering people is appropriate physical touch, such as touching a hand, arm, or foot when praying, giving a light hug, or physically helping them move to a chair. These efforts break down walls of insecurity and open greater opportunities for trust and ministry.

There is, however, a need for great discernment and for appropriate caution. The perception that physical touch brings can be mixed. This is why the nineteenth-century American pastor and trainer of pastors Samuel Miller shared these words for those ministering to the opposite sex:

> In a word, in all your associations with the other sex, let your delicacy be of the most scrupulous kind. Shun not only the reality, but even the appearance of evil. And remember that the very confidence, with respect to purity, which is commonly placed in a clergyman's character, while it is, in some respects, highly advantageous, may become a snare to him in a variety of ways easily conceivable.[13]

So, then, we must assess several issues to know what is appropriate and what is not. The age, gender, and type of relationship we have with the person determine how we should engage. For example, I am very comfortable holding the hand of the eighty-five-year-old widow, whom I know very well and who sees me as her grandson. I am not comfortable, however, with physically touching a female church member who is close to my age (married or single). Physical touch can be profoundly effective or damaging. Be wise in how you use it.

### Look a Person in the Eye

We rarely notice good, effective eye contact, that is, until we experience bad eye contact. Consider for a moment the importance of eye contact in casual conversation with someone. Good eye contact communicates interest in both the person and what is being said, while bad eye contact communicates disinterest, boredom, and presumed tension between both parties. These principles are magnified in a hospital room.

I once visited an anxious elderly widow in the hospital. She was very nervous, even when someone visited her in her home, so you can imagine how uncomfortable it was for her to have a visitor see her with uncombed hair, no makeup, and the "I haven't had a shower for days" look. I made sure I always looked her in the eye while I was there, because I knew she would be insecure about her appearance. I watched the walls of fear break down as I simply smiled, talked with her warmly, and always looked her in the eye.

Good eye contact immediately communicates you are interested in and comfortable with the other person. If you are visiting someone in a hospital or nursing home, they are already sensitive about their appearance. Many of them are attached to heart monitors or hooked up to IV machines pumping nourishment or medication. Bad eye contact will only heighten their already sensitive disposition toward their appearance. We should be disciplined with our eye contact in our conversations with others, especially when visiting those who are sick.

## Prepare Your Heart

First, we must prepare to visit others out of love, not duty. Do not underestimate the intuition of the sick. We often reveal by our manner whether our motivation is duty or love. This is the first heart issue we must honestly assess. It's easy for pastors to fall into the trap of thinking that visitation is one aspect of the job the church has hired us to do. Pastors must make a special effort to make sure they are visiting the sick out of love and care, not obligation. Curtis Thomas, a seasoned pastor of over forty years, writes, "Our visits should never appear only as professional duties. If the patient perceives that we are there only to carry out our responsibility, rather than having a genuine concern for him or her, our visit can do more harm than good."[14]

Next, we must prepare our hearts for what we might see and experience. Remember that we may be visiting someone who is dying, and there are disturbing realities that accompany death. We may see blood or tubes and needles placed into unthinkable places. Deep pain, gasping of breath, and many other mannerisms can make even the toughest person squeamish. However, these circumstances are not reasons to avoid caring for that person. In fact, these scenarios are wonderful moments given by God to force us to prepare our hearts as we rely completely on the Holy Spirit for strength.

Finally, more than simply preparing ourselves to avoid passing out when faced with these difficulties, we must spiritually prepare our hearts. Before we are face-to-face with the person we are visiting, we must have in mind the Scriptures we want to read; we must think through the words of encouragement and hope we intend to bring. Whatever promises of God we choose to share, we should remind ourselves of them, believe them, and allow them to fill our hearts with joy. That same intuition of the sick will then affirm they are receiving those words of truth from someone whose hope is also found in them.

## Conclusion

Charles Spurgeon is recognized as one of the most gifted, dedicated, brilliant, and impactful preachers and pastors in history. Most people give him this honorable distinction because of his piercing, articulate, Christ-centered, and gospel-driven sermons heard and read by thousands all over the world. Yet his faithfulness as a young pastor is often overlooked.

In 1854, at the tender age of twenty, Spurgeon moved to pastor a church in London (New Park Street Chapel), which later became the Metropolitan Tabernacle. Spurgeon had barely been in London twelve months when a severe case of cholera swept through London. Spurgeon recounts his efforts to care for the sick in the midst of horrific conditions:

> All day, and sometimes all night long, I went about from house to house, and saw men and women dying, and, oh, how glad they were to see my face! When many were afraid to enter their houses lest they should catch the deadly disease, we who had no fear about such things found ourselves most gladly listened to when we spoke of Christ and of things Divine.[15]

What an extraordinary example of a young, inexperienced pastor who feared God more than a contagious disease. What a model for us to see the sacrificial care Spurgeon gave at great risk because he knew of the spiritual fruit that could come only at the bedside of a dying man.

Spurgeon made visiting the afflicted a priority. Even as a young pastor, Spurgeon's gift to preach was evident to all who heard him, which brought great demand on his time. Yet Spurgeon placed all those opportunities aside: "During that epidemic of cholera, though I had many engagements in the country, I gave them up that I might remain in London to visit the sick and the dying."[16]

The demands on Spurgeon's life, even at twenty years of age, were great, quite possibly greater than the demands on most of us who live in one of the busiest cultures in history. We can certainly see through Spurgeon's example the significant impact that visiting the sick can have. However, what may be most applicable in this account is the sacrifices Spurgeon made to prioritize this divine task. He emphasizes that this priority is not only for pastors and leaders in the church but "for all who love souls."[17]

May we show our deep love for souls, specifically the souls of those with whom we have made a covenant in our local church. As we fellowship with, love, care for, and encourage one another, let us not lose sight of those who can easily be forgotten. Let us not forget those who do not fight for our attention, like so many other things in our lives do. We must take the initiative. The task of visiting the sick will not slip soundlessly into our schedules. However, take heart. When we are deliberate about visiting the sick and afflicted in our churches, we can trust that a divine task is being done, souls are being loved and nurtured on behalf of the Chief Shepherd, change is happening within us, the gospel is being revealed, and God is being glorified.

## Chapter 6

# Comfort the Grieving

**Therefore encourage one another with these words.**

**1 Thessalonians 4:18**

The hospital room and the funeral home are some of the best classrooms in which to learn pastoral ministry. I have held the hands of elderly saints and prayed over them as they took their last breath. I have won over my "enemies" because I took the time to visit them when they were in the hospital. I have watched despair turn to hope as I've sat with a grieving widow and talked about Christ. The hospital room and the funeral home present pastors with learning opportunities that can't be found elsewhere. Death reminds us of our frailty and our brokenness. It jolts our hearts out of the delusion of invincibility. Death restores our focus on the eternal things when we are daily tempted to live in the temporal. It compels us to acknowledge that our life is a vapor—here today, gone tomorrow.

Sadly, the places where we best learn how to speak to people about death are the places we tend to avoid—hospitals, nursing homes, and funeral homes. Why? Because ministry in these places is not glamorous. It requires an engagement of the heart that many are not comfortable pursuing on a regular basis. Talking with people in these situations creates burdens that are painful to bear. We won't gain public recognition. Most of the time, no one even knows we are making these visits, other than God and the people we visit. Yet this is the calling of a pastor. Pastors are responsible to care for those who are grieving. But how? How does a pastor effectively and compassionately care for those dealing with the pain of loss?

## Comfort with Biblical and Spiritual Realities

God is a God of comfort (Psalms 23:4; 57:1). God is faithful to care for and comfort his people during dark moments. Though there is much to learn from the way God comforted his people in the Old Testament, the best models of compassionate care for the grieving are those of Christ and his apostles.

### *Jesus Comforted the Grieving*

Jesus comforted those grieving the loss of loved ones. The most notable example is seen when Jesus went to comfort two sisters and close friends, Mary and Martha, as they grieved the loss of their brother, Lazarus. Mary and Martha had sent for Jesus, asking him to heal Lazarus, as they knew he had the power to do, but Jesus refused to come until it was too late. Lazarus succumbed to his illness and died. Several days later, Jesus arrived at his grave site:

> On his arrival, Jesus found that Lazarus had already been in the tomb for four days. Now Bethany was less than two miles from Jerusalem, and many Jews had come to Martha and Mary to comfort them in the loss of their brother. When Martha heard that Jesus was coming, she went out to meet him, but Mary stayed at home.
>
> "Lord," Martha said to Jesus, "if you had been here, my brother would not have died. But I know that even now God will give you whatever you ask."
>
> Jesus said to her, "Your brother will rise again."
>
> Martha answered, "I know he will rise again in the

resurrection at the last day."

Jesus said to her, "I am the resurrection and the life. The one who believes in me will live, even though they die; and whoever lives by believing in me will never die. Do you believe this?"

"Yes, Lord," she replied, "I believe that you are the Messiah, the Son of God, who is to come into the world."

**John 11:17 – 27**

Jesus knows Martha is grieving, but he doesn't shy away from speaking truth to her. He cares for Martha in her grief by reminding her of who he is. He comforts Martha by saying to her, "I am the resurrection and the life. The one who believes in me will live, even though they die; and whoever lives by believing in me will never die. Do you believe this?" (John 11:25 – 26). Jesus declares that he is the resurrection and the life. He reminds us in our greatest moments of sorrow and grief, especially when it comes to death, that our souls are comforted by the truth of who Jesus is in the face of death.

Lastly, Jesus asks a question, "Do you believe this?" Comfort is not found in bland assurances of hope. It comes from truly believing that Jesus is who he says he is. This is not just a nice saying; it is a real hope anchored in historical reality. Jesus has conquered death and provided salvation for those who believe in him. His power over death was demonstrated to these who watched him raise Lazarus from the grave and by his own resurrection on the third day after his death.

The comfort Jesus offers begins with the truth of who he is and what he has done, but it doesn't end there. The gospel of John continues:

After [Martha] had said this, she went back and called her sister Mary aside. "The Teacher is here," she said, "and is asking for you." When Mary heard this, she got up quickly and went to him ...

> When Mary reached the place where Jesus was and
> saw him, she fell at his feet and said, "Lord, if you had
> been here, my brother would not have died."
>
> When Jesus saw her weeping, and the Jews who
> had come along with her also weeping, he was deeply
> moved in spirit and troubled. "Where have you laid
> him?" he asked.
>
> "Come and see, Lord," they replied.
>
> Jesus wept.
>
> Then the Jews said, "See how he loved him!"
>
> **John 11:28–29, 32–36**

As we saw earlier, Jesus offers hope by reminding people of who he is and what he has done, but he also acknowledges the pain caused by death. Jesus grieved for and with the hurting, and we are told he was "deeply moved" and that he wept. Jesus likely wept for many reasons, but most commentators believe he was truly sad about the reality of death and the implications of what death brings. Death creates separation from loved ones. And that separation brings a deep sense of loss. Jesus grieved the death of Lazarus even as he knew he would soon raise him back to life. Jesus reminds us it is okay to weep and to feel deep emotion, even when we hold to the firm and sure hope of the resurrection. It is good to grieve when we face deep loss.

### Paul Comforted the Grieving

When he encountered the risen Christ on the road to Damascus, the apostle Paul found the hope that Jesus offers. Paul believed in the Lord Jesus Christ and was called to be an apostle. He would make several missionary journeys, planting churches throughout the Mediterranean and Asia Minor. In a letter to believers in Thessalonica, he offers comfort by explaining what happens when a believer dies:

> Brothers and sisters, we do not want you to be uninformed about those who sleep in death, so that you do not grieve like the rest of mankind, who have no hope. For we believe that Jesus died and rose again, and so we believe that God will bring with Jesus those who have fallen asleep in him. According to the Lord's word, we tell you that we who are still alive, who are left until the coming of the Lord, will certainly not precede those who have fallen asleep. For the Lord himself will come down from heaven, with a loud command, with the voice of the archangel and with the trumpet call of God, and the dead in Christ will rise first. After that, we who are still alive and are left will be caught up together with them in the clouds to meet the Lord in the air. And so we will be with the Lord forever. Therefore encourage one another with these words.      **1 Thessalonians 4:13–18**

Paul's purpose in sharing these words is clear. He does not want the Thessalonian believers to be "uninformed" and he knows that this knowledge of what happens to believers who die will bring encouragement to them. He makes it plain that anyone who is in Christ will be raised with Christ when the Lord returns. This includes both those who are alive at Christ's return and those who have already died. This knowledge should lead to a different kind of grieving from what non-Christians experience—a grief rooted in hope, not despair. These Christians in Thessalonica are to believe and speak these words to one another to encourage and comfort each other (1 Thessalonians 4:18). Paul teaches us that true comfort comes not just in believing who Jesus is but also in understanding God's purposes for the future, specifically, the resurrection he has secured for us.

Again, let me emphasize that true comfort isn't found in false words of sentiment or in clichés or platitudes. True comfort comes from actually believing the true words about Jesus and what he has done. As we've seen, comforting others with these truths does not require hiding our grief or a false stoicism. It involves being present to weep with those who weep and to hold forth Christ, who is the resurrection and the life.

## Comfort through the Funeral

Pastors are always preparing something. If they are not preaching, they are preparing to preach. If they are not leading a meeting, they are preparing to lead. Sermons and meetings have clear places on their calendar, with all kinds of reminders attached. Funerals don't work that way. They get dropped into the schedule unannounced and are challenging to prepare for two reasons.

First, funerals typically require a quick turnaround. Death comes when we least expect it and often at an inconvenient time. Normally, a pastor will have between two to five days to plan and prepare for a funeral. So a funeral gets crammed into the schedule for the week, and previously planned meetings are pushed back. Immediately, a pastor is forced to decide which tasks need to wait. It's important to think through some of this beforehand, long before the phone call comes. Funeral preparation begins with faithfully shepherding the lives of our people.

The second challenge is that every funeral is unique. You are immersing yourself in the life of a family that has been forever changed by a death. Every family has its own tensions, dysfunctions, and quirks, and all of these can be heightened during the grieving process. Pastors can quickly experience emotional and mental exhaustion as they walk with the family. Regardless of how well we are prepared (or not prepared), dependence on the Lord is essential. As we travel to the funeral home to be an ambassador of Christ, we must remind ourselves that our job is to make him central in all we do.

### Preservice Logistics

Plan to arrive at the funeral home fifteen to thirty minutes before the funeral starts. This allows you to greet the family, check in with the funeral director, and check to be sure plans haven't changed since the director last talked with you (because they often do change). This can also prevent one of the most embarrassing moments of your ministry—being late to conduct a funeral (trust me I know). Inform the funeral director at this time whether you will ride with him to the graveside or drive on your own in the procession. Make sure those involved in the service are accounted for and are prepared to participate as planned. Ideally, you will want to meet with all participants a few minutes before the service in order to talk through the details and pray that the Lord would awaken souls to the gospel and comfort his hurting people. Finally, make sure you start on time. Many folks have come early with the anticipation that the service will start when announced. Though there are exceptions, you should be able to count on the funeral director to help and not to hinder this timeliness.

Some funeral homes close the casket before the service begins. In one tradition, the minister is typically asked to meet for prayer with the family prior to the beginning of the funeral service. Often, if the casket is already in the chapel, the director will close the casket before the family enters. In other traditions, if the deceased has been lying in state in a family room, the minister will pray with the family, and then the family will be led to the chapel. Meanwhile, the minister waits with the casket as the directors close it. Then he leads the casket into the service, motioning for the attendees to stand in honor of the deceased. What's important is not so much the specific tradition, but making sure you know the typical protocol for that particular funeral home. Don't assume they all do it the same way.

### The Funeral Service

There is much to think about as you perform a funeral service. You have likely prepared some material and planned what to do and how to do it. Stand firmly on your decisions. As you facilitate

Pray sympathetically
Speak Eulogy compassionately
Exhort those grieving
Preach the Gospel

the funeral, make sure Christ and his saving work are on display throughout. Pray sympathetically. Speak the eulogy in a way you would want the person doing your eulogy to speak. Read God's word, knowing it is alive, active, and sharper than any double-edged sword, capable of piercing the deepest parts of our being (Hebrews 4:12). Exhort those who grieve, knowing how helpful that counsel once was to you. Preach the gospel and call people to respond to it, knowing faith comes from hearing the word about Christ (Romans 10:17). Then trust in God to do his mighty work by his Spirit according to his good and perfect will.

The opening words of a funeral service can feel as awkward as those first words we speak to the family that has just lost their loved one. The gathered audience will likely be more attentive than those on a normal Sunday. We must seize the opportunity to choose our words carefully, because they will set the tone for the entire service. Always allow God to speak before you do. Everyone in attendance is asking the question, "Why, God?" Choose a passage of Scripture that cuts through the questions, sorrow, and skepticism to declare the unchanging character of our great God.

God's words will always be more powerful, profound, and persuasive than our own. Begin by allowing God to pierce through the doubts by sharing from God's word. After you have prepared a welcome for those attending and state why you have gathered, shape the rest of the funeral service around five areas, asking how the gospel can be accurately portrayed in each of them: prayer, music, Scripture readings, eulogy, and sermon.[18]

1) Prayer
2) Music
3) Scripture Rdg
4) Eulogy
5) Sermon

Although adjustments will need to be made for the funeral of an unbeliever, you can still stick to these basic principles in your preparation. The gospel needs to be clear in these moments as well; however, discernment needs to be applied when the spiritual condition of the deceased is in question. It is unhelpful and unloving to preach the deceased into hell. The best advice I ever received about conducting a funeral service for both unbelievers and professing nominal believers is this: Don't preach them into heaven; don't preach them into hell. Just preach the gospel for the people who are there.[19]

Remember that you are not God. You cannot know with certainty the final spiritual condition of an individual, and this issue shouldn't be the focus of a funeral where these realities are uncertain. The funeral is for those present, for those who are hurting and grieving. Preach the gospel, help them grieve, and extend to them the hope of Christ.

### Postservice Logistics

After concluding the service, it is customary to stand at the head of the casket while the funeral director dismisses the attendees and gives directions. I find it helpful to position myself at the head of the casket to be available for those who would like to greet you, but not blocking the exit. I once co-led a funeral with a pastor who at the conclusion of the service placed himself not at the head of the casket but at the center of the door by which everyone had to exit. As I stood at the head of the casket, I watched many awkward moments of which this pastor was sadly unaware. Don't be surprised or offended if someone bypasses you. Often the attendees are led to the front to greet the emotional family and then walk to the casket to say their own final good-bye. However, some will want to greet you. Appear inviting. Speak warmly and kindly. Some of the most encouraging feedback I have heard after a funeral has been at that moment. Probably the most encouraging thing I ever hear in such moments, especially at a funeral for a non-Christian, is the comment of a person who comes over and says, "Thank you for preaching the gospel clearly."

After the attendees have been escorted from the room, the family is given their final moment with their loved one before the casket is closed (assuming it was still open). Remain in the room, but move from the vicinity of the casket so the family can have their time and space. Your presence in that moment will often be a source of great encouragement to the family. In typical protocol, once the family has been escorted outside, the funeral director closes the door to the room in order to close the casket. This prevents any unnecessary trauma to family members who would have a hard time seeing the casket shut. You will stay for the closing of the casket as the overseer of the proceedings, as well as the one who leads the casket to the waiting hearse.

Once the funeral director gives the signal, walk in front to lead the casket through the doors so the pallbearers can lift it into the hearse. You will proceed to the front car to ride with the funeral director (which I recommend), or you may get in your car to drive, which more than likely has been put in the proper position in the procession by a funeral home employee. If you ride with the director, you will be tempted to try to get a few tasks done during the slow, gentle journey to the grave site. However, it is beneficial to take advantage of this time to build a relationship with the director.

## The Graveside Service

Upon arrival at the grave site, walk to the back of the hearse, since you will be leading the casket to the grave. In the same way you led the casket to the hearse, you now walk in front of it to lead it to the grave. The grave site is typically marked with a canopy or some kind of visual cue that is easy to spot. However, if you have any doubts about where you are going, just ask the director. Be careful as you walk through uneven ground and maneuver through scattered graves to reach the open grave that awaits the deceased. You will stand at the head of the casket once it has been placed on the lowering device that holds it above the prepared grave.

I am not a fan of lengthy graveside services. You have just conducted a full funeral. The family is likely on the edge of emotional exhaustion, and often the conditions at the grave site are less than ideal. A pastor's portion of the graveside service should last no longer than five minutes. Keep in mind that any military ceremony or additional graveside logistics will follow your portion; these ceremonies can be lengthy, depending on how decorated the deceased was.

Our aim at a graveside is to reiterate the hope we have in Christ, which we preached at the funeral service. I typically find an introduction, Scripture reading, and final prayer reflecting on the passage read to be an appropriate, tasteful, and time-sensitive approach to a graveside service. For the deceased who was a believer in Christ, 1 Thessalonians 4:13–18 and 1 Corinthians 15:50–58 are fitting passages to read as words of encouragement and comfort for fellow believers that this body being committed to the ground will one day be raised to be with Christ forever. For those whose spiritual state at time of death is less clear, reading a more general passage of comfort (Psalm 23) is appropriate. Use the final prayer as a way to connect the spiritual reality that true comfort from God comes from trusting in the life, death, and resurrection of his Son. The funeral director will typically close the graveside service.

Regardless of the circumstances, make this truth known that the great Puritan John Flavel expressed in such poignant words: "O then, as you expect peace or rest in the chambers of death, get union with Christ. A grave with Christ is a comfortable place."[20]

I want to mention one final thing. A growing number of people today are choosing cremation over graveside burial. The reasons vary—convenience for the family, a tight budget, living in a place where a burial is involved and challenging, and many others. In the case of cremation, a graveside service will typically not take place. There is no physical body to view, grieve over, and bury. The funeral service will end, and everyone will be dismissed. Nonetheless, applying these graveside principles in the moments after the conclusion of a funeral service is good and appropriate and can lay the groundwork for future ministry.

## Postfuneral Pastoral Care

Before you leave the grave site, be ready to share comments of care with the family and friends. Don't be in a hurry to leave, but give yourself time to mingle. Remember, those who are present there are in the throes of grief. This may be the time when someone asks you about something you said in the service—perhaps something the Lord used to awaken him to his need for Christ. Don't underestimate how the Lord may open gospel opportunities in these moments before you leave. Have your business card or contact information to give to the family and anyone who asks to speak with you further.

Once you have mingled with graveside attendees for a few moments, approach immediate family members. This will often provide an opportunity for them to say thank you for serving them through the service. Be sure to pay your respects and offer your condolences one last time. Let them know of your willingness to be of service in the future. They typically won't take you up on it, but the kind gesture can be a comfort to them. It does leave the door open for future ministry with them, whether or not they are church members. *FOLLOW UP!!!*

Make a plan to touch base with the family within the next month to see how they are doing, especially if they are members of your church. The grieving process takes time for everyone. Trust that the Lord has been at work through your words throughout the entire process. Once life returns to a regular routine, the truths you spoke will more likely begin to take root and bear fruit. Call the family. Meet with them. Ask them how they are doing. Ask them how the grieving process is going and whether they've been able to grieve as those who have hope. Ask how Christ has been a comfort to them if they are a Christian, or if they're not, ask if they've considered your words about the gospel since the funeral. Ask if there is anything you can do for them now.

Involve other church members in postfuneral care as well; the family will feel more cared for by the body of Christ, not just their pastor. Often, it is in the weeks and even months that follow where the hard sowing of the gospel seed through the funeral process begins to bear fruit. Try to be there for the harvest.

Finally, say good-bye to the funeral director before leaving. Make sure you encourage him if he handled the details well on his end and made the experience more comfortable for you. Don't forget that the director is serving this family with the same hope that they will feel cared for by his efforts. Encourage him if appropriate. Offer your services in the future, as all funeral homes are looking for pastors to fill in when other pastors are unavailable.

## Conclusion

Because a funeral has so many elements and logistics to prepare for, it is not uncommon for a pastor to have all his words prepared, the service planned out, everyone in place, and processional details checked off, and then to realize that an essential element had been neglected, namely, the pastor's heart. Do not become enslaved to the tyranny of funeral preparation, only to stand and carry it all out with an empty, drained, and calloused heart. Do not underestimate the emotional and mental strain involved in comforting the grieving while preparing and performing a funeral. Take note of three areas where the pastor must take time to prepare his heart, mind, and soul.

*1. Prepare for the unexpected.* Just when you think you've seen it all, the next funeral reveals you haven't. Even if you have seen fights break out, arrests made, uncontrollable wailing, fainting spells of family members and pallbearers, caskets dropped and knocked over, shouting conflicts between families and funeral directors, or funeral attire that would make most people blush, these experiences do not mean the next funeral will mirror these experiences. Because of this, prepare to see *anything*. Prepare to get the craziest response to something you say. Prepare to watch families at their worst. If you do this, you will be able to think clearly and wisely when the unexpected happens.

*2. Prepare to minister God's word.* Though there is much to manage, administrate, and facilitate, you are not the concierge of the funeral. You are a minister of God's word and a preacher of the gospel of Jesus Christ. Prepare your heart, mind, and soul in whatever way is necessary, so that when you stand before people at the beginning of the funeral service, you stand to minister God's word, trusting that God will work mightily through his word.

*3. Prepare to extend the hope of Christ.* You are not there to solve family conflicts or to help the funeral home learn how to function more smoothly. You are there to clearly present to each person the hope we have of forgiveness of sins and victory over death because of Christ. You can best prepare by thinking about who will be at the funeral service. Consider what kinds of questions you could ask the family to assess their spiritual condition as you talk with them. Prepare questions ahead of time from the words you have prepared to share, so that gospel opportunities can be unveiled in those conversations.

Wearing your administrator and facilitator cap throughout the process is necessary. It will serve as a helpful companion to maneuver through all the details and demands that accompany funerals. Nevertheless, you are ultimately a pastor and evangelist who is called on by the Chief Shepherd to prepare and conduct funerals as "a dying man preaching to dying men."[21] Prepare and conduct funerals in the knowledge that the grieving are hurting and are longing for tender care, as you remind them that they must look to Jesus as their only hope.

## Chapter 7

# Care for Widows

> Give proper recognition to those widows who are
> really in need. **1 Timothy 5:3**

We see some exciting and encouraging evidences that Jesus Christ is at work in his church through his Spirit. We are experiencing a recovery of biblical preaching. Churches are raising the bar of membership by recovering the practice of church discipline. The gospel is being clearly preached, and intentional plans to disciple new converts are being created. Churches are launching fruitful mercy ministries with proactive efforts to care for the poor, adopt orphans, and assist the homeless, hurting, and oppressed. The Lord continues to build his church in our day, and these are just a few of the many signs that he is at work.

However, there are several areas that are not recovering as quickly, if at all. Strong gospel preaching in some circles appears to be a reaction to the crushing effects of legalism in the church, yet this could squeeze out a rigorous pursuit of holiness in the next generation. And the fresh emergence of intentional mercy ministries in the church has led to a greater level of care for orphans, the poor, and the oppressed, as well as several other groups of hurting people. But there is a notable exception. When was the last time you heard someone talk about the importance of caring for widows?

It may seem strange to devote an entire chapter to this task in a book on pastoral ministry. But if it does seem strange, I believe it says more about our cultural priorities than anything else. So my goal here is to point out the biblical imperatives given to pastors and to God's people to care for widows and then to give a few practical suggestions for how pastors and church leaders can best fulfill this ministry.

## Caring for Widows: A Biblical Call?

Widows are largely neglected and forgotten about in the church today. Surely there are exceptions, but it is difficult to argue against the fact that our culture is infatuated with youth. Large portions of the evangelical church seem to be unaware of the biblical call to care for widows, even as they embrace ministry to the fatherless and the poor. Even among those who recognize widows as a distinct group identified in Scripture, many churches still do not make this ministry a priority.

### God's Desire

Austin Walker provides the best definition of a widow I've seen and articulates well the unique challenges a widow faced in the ancient days of Israel:

> A widow is a married woman whose husband has died and who remains unmarried. In the Bible mourning, weeping, and a sense of desolation, disillusionment, bitterness, loneliness, and helplessness were often experienced by a widow following the death of her spouse. The loss of a husband was often a social and economic tragedy. Falling into debt and poverty sometimes, but not always, resulted once the main source of her financial support had been removed. Becoming a widow made her vulnerable. She was frequently placed alongside similar people such as the stranger (the landless immigrant) and the fatherless (e.g., Exodus 22:21–22; Deuteronomy 24:17–21). Her plight would be aggravated if she had no able-bodied children to help her work the land of her former husband. Because of these changed

114

circumstances, widows were often marginalized. Therefore it is not surprising to find in ancient Israel that they were regarded as being in need of special protection.[22]

Widows are called out for special care among God's people throughout Old Testament times. While God promised to care for his chosen people, the Israelites, he also made promises of provision and care for specific people — for those with unique needs. The psalmist says the Lord is "a father to the fatherless, a defender of widows" (Psalm 68:5). Orphans and widows in particular had a special place in the heart of God, and this is reflected in numerous places throughout the first five books of the Bible. That care is powerfully seen in some of the narrative accounts of the Old Testament. In the book of Ruth, we witness God's care for Ruth, the childless widow, as he blesses her with redeeming favor in her marriage to Boaz, placing her in direct lineage to King David and ultimately the Messiah, Jesus Christ. The prophet Jeremiah speaks of God's care for widows, even those from other nations. Speaking of Edom, Jeremiah quotes God as saying, "Leave your fatherless children; I will keep them alive. Your widows too can depend on me" (Jeremiah 49:11).

These are just a few examples, yet they reveal the compassion God had on those facing this painful bereavement. God also directly calls his people, through various laws, to care for the foreigner, fatherless, and widow (Deuteronomy 24:19).

## The Church's Calling

The book of Acts reveals several key incidents in the early church that help us understand how the early followers of Christ lived out the Old Testament emphasis on caring for the widow. Was this a ministry they gave priority to, or did they move on to other concerns?

One of the best examples of their approach to caring for widows is found in Acts 6:1–7. The apostles had become aware that certain widows in the church were not being properly cared for.

Recognizing this as a significant issue, they instructed church leaders to appoint seven godly men filled with the Holy Spirit to take charge of caring for the widows. Often, I've heard pastors use this passage to teach about leadership or to give insight into the offices of the church and the roles of pastors and deacons (1 Timothy 3:1–14). Commonly overlooked, though, is the actual task these Spirit-filled men were assigned. The first task—their primary responsibility—was to make sure widows in the early church, who were being overlooked in the daily servings of food, were receiving adequate care. Luke felt this incident was important for us to know and understand, and so he included it in his history of the early church when he wrote Acts. Clearly, caring for widows was a priority in the early church.

Did this priority fade as the church grew and expanded into other cultures? In his letter to Timothy, Paul asks Timothy to make sure intentional care for widows remained a priority in the church (1 Timothy 5:3–16). In fact, Paul dedicates most of that chapter to giving detailed instructions on this matter. He explains who qualifies as a widow, addresses different circumstances widows might be facing, and gives advice on how churches should intentionally care for widows in those situations. Paul wanted Timothy to see that caring for widows was still an indispensable priority in church. Shouldn't this priority of the early church remain a priority today?

In addition to Paul and Peter, James highlights this ministry, even defining pure religion acceptable to God as this: "to look after orphans and widows in their distress and to keep oneself from being polluted by the world" (James 1:27). James focuses attention on the works of the Christian life that reflect true faith and pure religion in God's sight, and caring for widows and orphans is offered as an inarguable priority. All pastors of the gospel of the Lord Jesus Christ should heed these commands and seek to actively engage in caring for widows. But what does that mean? How does a pastor engage in this ministry?

## Pastoral Tools to Care for Widows

The Bible is filled with examples of God's care for the widow and Christ's commands, through his apostles, for his church to minister to widows. Yet even many biblically astute pastors may not see these imperatives, much less know how to care for the needs of widows. They are not aware of the intense waves of loneliness and despair a widow can experience in the various stages of grief. To minister to widows, you'll need some help. Here are a few suggestions to prepare you to intentionally minister in the face of the unique challenges that widows face.*

### *Minister the Word*

Pastors can begin by showing a widow, biblically, that it is God's desire to provide care for her. Read through a few passages that speak specifically to God's care, including Scriptures that address specific needs and challenges, and then be sure to pray for those needs. Prepare by selecting a few passages that speak into the loneliness and despair a widow may be experiencing. Ask questions about how she is doing. Her responses will guide you toward what else to share. I find it helpful to think about passages in various categories. Consider these five areas, with verses that may be helpful, depending on the situation you are dealing with:

- **Passages of comfort especially for widows:** Psalms 23; 28; 34; 46; 62; 68:5; 113; Jeremiah 49:11; Hebrews 4:14–16

- **Passages that show God's intentional care for widows:** Deuteronomy 16:11; Ruth 1–4; 1 Kings 17; Psalm 146:9; Lamentations 1:1–2; Luke 7:12–13; Acts 6:1–7; 1 Timothy 5:1–10

---

*Much of the practical section of this chapter is found in the extensive forthcoming work on the subject by Brian Croft and Austin Walker titled *Caring for Widows*.

- **Succinct gospel passages:** John 11:25–26; Romans 5:6–11; 2 Corinthians 5:17–21; Ephesians 2:1–10
- **Passages dealing with the purpose of suffering for the believer:** 2 Corinthians 12:7–9; James 1:2–4; 1 Peter 1:6–7; 4:12–19
- **Passages related to the reality and hope of eternity with Christ:** John 10:27–30; 14:1–3; Philippians 1:21–23; 1 Peter 1:3–5

Having such a list or even a few passages in mind will enable you to be better equipped as you deal with the range of emotions widows experience—emotions that range from sorrow to anger. Above all, don't forget your Bible. Whatever passage you choose for that moment, pray in line with the truths of that passage. As you do so, you will reiterate the truths from Scripture you have just read and keep a singular focus on what you hope this hurting widow retains after your visit is over.

### Listen and Learn

It was no secret. Everyone knew Mrs. Tillie Roberts was one of my favorite widows to visit. Tillie Roberts lived to be 106 years old, and she died just three months shy of her next birthday. Even in her final days, she had a mind like a steel trap. She drove herself to church until the age of 103. She had been widowed for over forty years and had never remarried, continuing to live in her home alone. She would often run into my wife and our four children at the grocery store and would always remember their names and birthdays! She loved Jesus. She loved our church. She was always kind and supportive of me as her pastor. She was an amazing woman.

As I visited with her throughout the years, Tillie taught me a lot of things. Among the most important were the disciplines of *listening* and *learning*. I'm something of a history buff, and this woman had lived almost four times the life I had lived! There was much for me to learn. Only a fool would not listen and learn from this seasoned woman of God.

## Listen

When caring for a widow, especially as you sit with her in her home, begin by listening to her story. Ask her about her life. Allow her to tell stories about her childhood. Ask about her life with her husband—and listen. Ask her how they met and how she knew she was supposed to marry him. Ask about their early years of marriage and the financial challenges they faced at different points in their life—then listen. Ask about their children and grandchildren and the ways she was blessed to have them in her life. Ask about the way she and her husband made a living and the different places they lived. Ask about her home; have her give you a tour and help you become immersed in her world. The décor in her home likely represents something special and important. Listen as she shares.

Be sure to listen to her spiritual journey too. Ask her about her walk with Christ. Ask her about her testimony and when she came to see her need for Jesus—listen and rejoice. Ask her about the church she grew up in and her history with the church you pastor—and listen. Ask her what passages from God's word are most meaningful to her. Ask her about those who may have discipled her and why those relationships were so meaningful. Ask her about her sufferings and how her faith sustained her through them—listen carefully. Ask and listen. Listening is a gift that allows her to sense the value God places on her life and to recall all that the Lord has done for her. It provides a healthy avenue for her to continue the grieving process and a chance for you to learn about her life and get to know her better.

## Learn

What do we learn as we listen to widows? Few moments in life provide the clarity and perspective that come when a person experiences deep loss. The loss of a spouse is certainly one of those moments. As you ask questions and listen, you will learn about this precious saint entrusted to your care. You will learn about her life — her joys and struggles, the sufferings she has endured, her painful losses and her exciting victories. You will learn about her faith — how Christ saved her, how Christ walked with her through sufferings, how Christ has ministered grace to her throughout her life, and even things about your church you may not know.

But if you ask the right questions and listen well, you will learn not only about her and about her life, but about your own as well. Because most widows have experienced suffering and have persevered through strong faith in Jesus Christ, trusting in the sovereign goodness of God, their outlook on life often contains a wealth of wisdom and faith. It is tragic that many pastors look at elderly members as burdens weighing down the congregation and keeping it from moving forward. Elderly widows are some of the church's most insightful people to listen to and learn from because they have endured. Their faith throughout the decades has remained steadfast.

There was much I learned from spending time listening to Tillie Roberts. Whenever I visited her in her home, she shared pictures and stories of special furniture and places in her home where she had fallen. She spoke of her enduring faith in Jesus. I heard stories of the Great Depression, learned what life was like without cars, planes, television, or the Internet. She was the only person I knew who could explain the ancient farming tools hanging on the walls at Cracker Barrel. When I conducted her funeral, I recalled all that I had learned from her — especially the stories from her life that have equipped me to care for others better and have made me a wiser pastor. Her enduring faith challenged me to strive for the same faithfulness in my own life. These were special moments, but they don't happen easily or immediately. They take time. Time spent listening and learning.

## Provide a Gift

Everyone loves receiving a gift. Some love gifts more than others, but almost everyone appreciates the sentiment behind a gift. A gift says, "I love and appreciate you." It communicates thoughtfulness and intentionality. Giving a gift to a widow can be a particularly encouraging gesture for them. Widows were once wives, and many of them are mothers and grandmothers. Many have made sacrificial efforts to give gifts to others, and they know what a gift means. A widow, just like anyone else, will be uniquely encouraged by gifts that speak to a certain need they have. I often think in three categories: a needed gift, an edible gift, and a sentimental gift. I try to think of things that will uniquely minister to her. Deacons in the local church can help with gathering and distributing these gifts to meet these physical and emotional needs and in this way be the same kind of servants who were set apart in the early church for this task (Acts 6:1–7).

## A Needed Gift

Have you ever heard someone say, "I need to get that new phone" or "I need to see that movie as soon as it comes out on Blu-ray"? Sometimes we convince ourselves these are things we truly need. But often, they are nothing more than wants camouflaged as needs. A needed gift is something that addresses a real need, something a widow requires so she can persevere in her daily life. For example, in our church we have an international refugee, a widow who has several children. She isn't particularly concerned with having the latest and greatest phone (though she very likely needs a phone); she simply wants to know what her children will eat for that day. She doesn't care about what's playing at the movie theater down the street; she wonders if the landlord is going to evict her from her apartment. Many widows have many real needs that a pastor can encourage his church to help meet. A gift that meets an immediate need is a very biblical way to serve a widow. It can act as a great encouragement as she sees God's provision through his church.

In the winter months as the weather gets cold, older people tend to have several specific needs. They may need help keeping up their property, salting the sidewalks or shoveling snow off the driveway. The longer, darker, and colder nights can heighten depression and increase feelings of loneliness. You can provide for the physical needs of widows by mowing lawns, raking leaves, cleaning gutters, providing rides to and from church or doctor's appointments, changing lightbulbs, or just doing household maintenance inside the home. Surprising them with these unexpected acts of service is a particularly sweet gift.

### An Edible Gift

Not all widows have financial or physical needs. A wise husband may have invested money before he died to make sure his wife will be cared for; the widow herself may be skilled at managing her resources. And another knickknack to clutter the fireplace mantel may be the last thing you want to bring. Instead, do some research and find out what goodies she loved to make for herself and her husband and children. Bake a treat or buy one, and bring it to her on your next visit. Find out if she has a favorite coffee or tea, and wrap it in a package with a nice bow and deliver it to her. One Christmas, my wife made special chocolates with our young children. They then made special deliveries to each of the elderly widows in our congregation. A widow may not have immediate physical needs, but you can always find ways to brighten her day and remind her she is not forgotten.

### A Sentimental Gift

The most meaningful gifts I have received are the ones made just for me. I think of the cards my young children made for me or the thoughtful, handwritten cards from my wife. In other cases, it might be a ticket to a sporting event from a friend who remembered how much I wanted to be there. The gifts that communicate thoughtfulness are the most meaningful, and gifts for widows are no different. One of the best approaches is to find out what kinds of sentimental gifts a widow's husband used to give her, and you may be able to find something similar that will lift her spirits because they'll remind her of the way her husband used to love her and allow her to experience that love yet again through the love of her church family.

Ministering grace to a widow with a gift is about more than just the gift; it is also about the message you communicate by giving the gift. Do your homework! Find out what her physical needs are. Or bake some goodies. Or simply have your children make a card that tells them you appreciate them. Gifts like these are often used by God in ways you cannot know or anticipate. Such gifts can powerfully remind a widow that she is not forgotten.

## Involve Your Wife and Family

One of the most difficult funerals I ever conducted was that of a young father and husband, a man who was a deacon in our church. This dear friend was killed in a car crash, leaving behind his wife and children. During this very painful time for his family, my wife played an essential role in caring for this shocked widow as she experienced deep grief. As a pastor, don't assume you need to minister alone. Even more importantly, don't assume you *can* minister alone. If you have a family, God will often use your family to bring blessing and comfort to those you minister to in the church.

Pastors call on their wives for many things—leading the Sunday school class when the teacher called in sick or bringing an extra dish to the church potluck, for example. But even more significant is the role your wife can play when ministering to other women who are in crisis. This is especially true when you meet with a new widow. Whether it is a young widow who suddenly lost her husband or an older woman who lost her husband of fifty years, your wife is an invaluable resource as you care for these widows. And often she can model and encourage other women in the church to serve in a similar way.

Your wife's care for older widows provides a great role model for a younger woman to care for an older woman. Elderly widows appreciate care from anyone in the church, but they especially love care from younger women. I have heard many older widows share that it feels similar to receiving care from a daughter, even if they never had a daughter of their own.

As younger women become involved, God also provides an opportunity for an older woman to instruct and encourage a younger woman, following the biblical pattern in Titus 2:3–4. These interactions can be profoundly helpful to a younger woman as she gains wise instruction and perspective on life from an older woman. Not every woman has had this opportunity, and many find they are blessed by the experience. In our church, we have an elderly widow in her midnineties who was married for more than fifty years and had seven children, including a set of twins. This woman is a wonderful resource of wisdom and insight for the young women, wives, and moms in our church. Younger women in the church have much to learn from women like these. And these elderly widows love using their many years of experience to serve Christ's people.

When it comes to younger widows, a pastor's wife can be a special friend, a companion, and a wise accountability partner. We pastors need to be intentional about involving our wives in caring for younger widows, not just for the companionship they provide, but to help us avoid becoming ensnared in dangerous situations as we spend time ministering to vulnerable women struggling with emotional and spiritual challenges brought on by their loss. I wish it hadn't happened, but I've seen a pastor leave his wife to marry a younger widow from his congregation. Though most pastors care with the best of intentions, we must remember no one is above temptation, and pastors must guard their lives and their hearts by avoiding potentially compromising situations. They should never underestimate the emotions that can be stirred in these moments, and a particular guard needs to be in place when caring for hurting widows. A pastor's wife can assist in ministering closely in these situations, allowing us to care for the young women while remaining above reproach.

Caring for widows, both young and old, can be one of the most rewarding and significant roles a pastor's wife can play, but it does not need to exclusively depend on her involvement. Her participation will often invite other women, wives, and moms in the local church to engage in the same way. Sometimes small groups of women will gather for fellowship. Encourage your wife to be involved in these ministries if she is able and willing. And encourage other women to join to make sure the burden of ministry doesn't rest too heavily on her alone.

Never underestimate the impact children can have in the lives of others as well. I once conducted the funeral of a beloved widow in our church, and I was reminded of the blessings of having older people connected to our youth and of the positive influence older widows can have on our children. When I brought my family to her funeral, we were greeted by members of this woman's family. We had never met them before, but somehow they knew my children's names and talked about them and about her love for them. The family was excited to meet the children their loved one had talked about. And I began to realize just how much my children had helped me in caring for this woman through the years. The expressions of love from her family showed they had brought her joy in a way I could never have done through my visits alone. This older woman dearly loved children, but she had never had any of her own. Yet she loved mine. In fact, this was one of the many reasons I loved and appreciated this woman.

Those of us who are parents know that children are a gift from God. Yet we can sometimes forget that our children are also a gift to our church family—if we are willing to share them. Every church has elderly widows who genuinely rejoice when a church member comes to visit them and brings their kids along for the visit.

In addition, these experiences are good for children. There is great benefit for a child to learn to love and to grieve. I saw this as we drove away from a visitation and my two oldest daughters, ages seven and ten at the time, began to cry. I don't like to see my daughters cry, but it reminded me that my children had genuine affection for this woman. They had learned to love, and now they were learning how to grieve. Parents mistakenly want to shelter their children from exposure to death when they are younger, yet a moment like this is a wonderful gift from God that helps our children understand its reality. Teach your children how to be grateful to God that they knew these special people and how to put their ultimate hope and trust in the gospel.

Finally, involving your children in caring for widows and the elderly will help them (and the older people in your church) to appreciate their need for one another. Sadly, the multigenerational local church is fading away in many places today. But this should not be. The best way to battle age segregation in the church is to intentionally do things that bring young and old together to grow in Christian love and affection for each other. I was deeply grateful for the way this widow, who had never had her own children, had faithfully loved so many children in our church just as if they were her own.

Children are not a burden to our ministry. On the contrary, they are a valuable gift from God to us. Sure, it may require a bit more planning and intentionality to include them in ministry, but the benefits are well worth the cost.

### Adopt during Holidays

The holidays are times of joy for many people, but they can also be times of great sadness for others. Widows, in particular, often struggle with memories and with feelings of sorrow during these times of the year. For a widow, Christmas, Thanksgiving, birthdays, and anniversaries are all reminders that her husband is gone. In the busyness of holiday seasons, family members are often preoccupied with other things and forget this can be a sad or discouraging time for their loved one. Widows are sometimes forgotten in the hustle and bustle of the event or season. Pastors, deacons, and church members can serve widows by adopting them for a time, including them in your own family's holiday plans.

One of the best ways to honor widows during the holiday season is to have a special dinner for them. I know of a pastor and his wife who planned a large potluck dinner at their church just to honor the widows at Christmas. Since many of them did not have family around at the time, it was a great way to remind them that the body of Christ is their family. In addition to the meal, you can provide small gifts, cards, or other treats that remind the women that they are loved, valued, and honored. You can also honor them by making them the focus of your prayer time during your public gatherings. One of our church's activities is to caravan around on a Saturday evening close to Christmas and visit elderly widows' homes. We sing Christ-honoring Christmas songs, and entire families join in for a great time of fellowship. The widows in our church are encouraged and lifted up by these visits. They are warmed by the fellowship and reminded that Christ has not forgotten them, and Christ's people haven't either.

Perhaps you will want to invite a widow to a Thanksgiving or Christmas dinner with your family. As I think about my own years as a child, the Thanksgiving and Christmas dinners that stick out the most are those when an elderly widow suddenly joined us for dinner—someone my father invited to our house at the last minute. I can only imagine what a blessing this was for these lonely women who had a meal with our family instead of sitting at home alone.

Never underestimate your opportunities to bless and encourage widows, especially during the holidays. If you step out of your comfort zone in these simple ways, I know you will not regret the fellowship you will experience with these dear saints. Our merciful God has adopted each of us into his eternal family through the precious blood of Jesus. Here is a wonderful opportunity to mirror that grace and highlight our eternal adoption by welcoming an older woman into your home for the holidays.

## Conclusion

If pastors want their ministry to mirror the heart of God *and* the ministry of the early church, then caring for widows is essential. Understanding the commands of Scripture is not enough. Proper, effective care for widows requires thoughtful evaluation of the unique needs of each widow. Remember that while other ministries will clamor for your attention, widows will typically not fight for your time and attention. Caring for them and making them a priority in your ministry will only happen as God speaks to your heart and moves you to respond in faith and obedience. But this doesn't mean you won't be blessed. Some of your most rewarding ministry will be experienced as you care for the widows in your church.

part 3

# faithfulness

# Chapter 8
# Confront Sin

"If your brother sins, go and show him his fault in private. If he listens to you, you have won your brother. But if he does not listen to you, take one or two more with you, so that 'by the mouth of two or three witnesses every fact may be confirmed.' If he refuses to listen to them, tell it to the church; and if he refuses to listen even to the church, let him be to you as a Gentile and a tax collector."                    **Matthew 18:15–17 NASB**

There are times when speaking the truth will hurt someone, but if we believe the truth has the power to set us free, then the best thing you can say to someone is a word that will bring conviction to their heart. None of us like to say words that might hurt someone, but often these are exactly what that person needs to find hope and healing. Charles Spurgeon's mother modeled this for her son when he was a young, rebellious child. Reflecting back on this experience, Spurgeon writes these words:

> It was the custom, on Sunday evenings, while we were yet little children, for [Mother] to stay at home with us, and then we sat round the table, and read verse by verse, and she explained the Scripture to us. After that was done, then came the time of pleading; there was a little piece of Alleine's *Alarm*, or of Baxter's *Call to the Unconverted*, and this was read with pointed observations made to each of us as we sat round the table; and the question was asked, how long it would be before we would think

about our state, how long before we would seek the Lord. Then came a mother's prayer, and some of the words of that prayer we shall never forget, even when our hair is grey. I remember, on one occasion, her praying thus: "Now Lord, if my children go on in their sins, it will not be from ignorance that they perish, and my soul must bear a swift witness against them at the day of judgment if they lay not hold of Christ." That thought of a mother's bearing swift witness against me, pierced my conscience, and stirred my heart.[23]

A faithful parent doesn't just say what a child *wants* to hear; a faithful parent says what a child *needs* to hear. They speak the truth to them for their long-term growth. And shepherds of God's sheep are no different than faithful parents. A faithful pastor must be willing to do and say the hard things his flock needs to be mature and stay healthy.

This is one of the most difficult tasks for the modern, busy pastor. Few pastors look forward to confronting sin in others. Often, then, this responsibility is ignored—and yet it cannot be ignored for long. All Christians battle sin. All pastors battle sin. And this is the reality we will face until Jesus returns for us. This does not mean we are called to confront any and every sin we witness in the life of another person. We are not called to police others, watching them until they fail and then we hurry to confront them.

No, there is a reason behind our call to confront. We confront sin out of love for God, for the person sinning, and for our church. We confront sin to honor the name of Christ in the hope that speaking the truth will lead to repentance and restoration. Confronting sin is something all Christians engage in with others in their relationships, but it is needed in a special way when Christians fall into sinful patterns and no longer are resolved to battle these sins or repent of them. The process of correction in these situations is known as church discipline. And pastors must lead the local church in engaging this task. In this chapter, we will look at what the Bible teaches about the responsibility of local churches in conducting church discipline, and then we'll look at some of the ways pastors should lead their churches in this process.

## Biblical Areas for Pastoral Intervention

The New Testament gives clear guidance for confronting sin in a Christian's life and provides a few ways to approach the process, depending on the particular circumstance we face.

### Unrepentant Sin

The process for confronting someone comes from Jesus himself. Jesus gives us a clear process to follow if we find a brother or sister in Christ who is unrepentant toward certain sins in their life, especially sins against others:

> "If your brother sins, go and show him his fault in private. If he listens to you, you have won your brother. But if he does not listen to you, take one or two more with you, so that 'by the mouth of two or three witnesses every fact may be confirmed.' If he refuses to listen to them, tell it to the church; and if he refuses to listen even to the church, let him be to you as a Gentile and a tax collector."　　　**Matthew 18:15 – 17 NASB**

Here is the three-step process of church discipline we should use when confronting a brother or sister in Christ:

*Step 1:* If they sin against you, admonish them in private. If they listen to you, you have won them over.

*Step 2:* If they don't listen, take two or three witnesses with you. Then if they continue to refuse to listen, tell it to the church.

*Step 3:* If they refuse to listen even to the church, treat them as you would a pagan or a tax collector.

The goal of church discipline is clear: to win your brother or sister in Christ back to a God-honoring lifestyle. This individual is living in open sin, doesn't care, and won't listen to anyone who confronts them about it. In this situation, speaking God's truth to them and confronting them are, in reality, loving acts. Allowing a person to live in open rebellion against God without warning them is not loving. So Jesus calls us to confront them in love to win them back. But this is not easy! As a shepherd, your sheep will not willingly engage in this unless you lead them through it.

## A Lack of Discipline

The church of Thessalonica was a model of a faithful church in so many ways. Yet some believers among them were not living out their transformation in Christ. The apostle Paul writes to this church about those individuals and how to identify them:

> Now we command you, brethren, in the name of our Lord Jesus Christ, that you keep away from every brother who leads an unruly life and not according to the tradition which you received from us. For you yourselves know how you ought to follow our example, because we did not act in an undisciplined manner among you, nor did we eat anyone's bread without paying for it, but with labor and hardship we kept working night and day so that we would not be a burden to any of you; not because we do not have the right to this, but in order to offer ourselves as a model for you, so that you would follow our example. For even when we were with you, we used to give you this order: if anyone is not willing to work, then he is not to eat, either. For we hear that some among you are leading an undisciplined life, doing no work at all, but acting like busybodies. Now such persons we command and exhort in the Lord Jesus Christ to work in quiet fashion

and eat their own bread. But as for you, brethren, do not
grow weary of doing good.

　　If anyone does not obey our instruction in this letter,
take special note of that person and do not associate
with him, so that he will be put to shame. Yet do not
regard him as an enemy, but admonish him as a brother.

**2 Thessalonians 3:6 – 15 NASB**

The apostle is not addressing here those with legitimate physical needs who are unable to provide for themselves. Paul is speaking about people in the church who are taking advantage of the generosity of the church. Apparently, some Thessalonian believers were capable of working and providing for their needs, but they were refusing to work and mooching off wealthier members. Paul commands the church to confront the sin of laziness and the exploitation of the church. While they were not working, these lazy Christians were meddling in other people's affairs, leading to sin. Paul urges the church to discipline those who are unwilling to work, and he details how these people will be won over through this confrontation.

### Divisiveness

In another letter, Paul writes to his young protégé, Titus, and encourages him to exercise church discipline, following a process similar to the one Jesus taught (Matthew 18:15 – 17), as he labors to establish churches in Crete. Paul instructs Titus to be aware of those who are harmfully divisive and to confront them in this way:

　　But avoid foolish controversies and genealogies
and arguments and quarrels about the law, because
these are unprofitable and useless. Warn a divisive
person once, and then warn them a second time. After
that, have nothing to do with them. You may be sure
that such people are warped and sinful; they are self-
condemned.　　　　　　　　　　　　　　**Titus 3:9 – 11**

Paul's words to Titus mirror the words of Jesus. When confronting someone in their sin, we have a process to follow that helps to determine if this person is truly converted. As Paul says, we warn that person once and then a second time. If they refuse to repent, Paul writes, "have nothing to do with them." This process reveals that "such people are warped and sinful; they are self-condemned." Paul teaches that the process of church discipline can help reveal the true state of a person's soul.

## Public and Scandalous Sin

In twenty years of pastoral ministry, one of my most painful experiences was learning one of our members had been physically abusing his wife. Another pastor and I met with the couple, and it was a heartbreaking, very messy situation. The man was unrepentant and unresponsive to our confrontation. Our meeting with the couple eventually led to a special members' meeting of the church, a public meeting at which we immediately removed this individual from church membership. In removing him from the church, we made a public statement about his actions, condemning them and letting others know his actions and lifestyle were inconsistent with those of a person who knows Christ.

In light of the previous examples, you may wonder, *Why the immediate removal of this individual?* For guidance, we looked to another public and awful situation Paul addressed in the Corinthian church—a church filled with arrogant and divisive members. These people had harshly judged Paul and other leaders in the church and had shown they valued the world more than Christ. In their arrogance they had overlooked a gross sinfulness that existed in the church—an action that could not be tolerated or ignored:

> It is actually reported that there is immorality among you, and immorality of such a kind as does not exist even among the Gentiles, that someone has his

father's wife. You have become arrogant and have not mourned instead, so that the one who had done this deed would be removed from your midst.

For I, on my part, though absent in body but present in spirit, have already judged him who has so committed this, as though I were present. In the name of our Lord Jesus, when you are assembled, and I with you in spirit, with the power of our Lord Jesus, I have decided to deliver such a one to Satan for the destruction of his flesh, so that his spirit may be saved in the day of the Lord Jesus.

Your boasting is not good. Do you not know that a little leaven leavens the whole lump of dough? Clean out the old leaven so that you may be a new lump, just as you are in fact unleavened. For Christ our Passover also has been sacrificed. Therefore let us celebrate the feast, not with old leaven, nor with the leaven of malice and wickedness, but with the unleavened bread of sincerity and truth.

I wrote you in my letter not to associate with immoral people; I did not at all mean with the immoral people of this world, or with the covetous and swindlers, or with idolaters, for then you would have to go out of the world. But actually, I wrote to you not to associate with any so-called brother if he is an immoral person, or covetous, or an idolater, or a reviler, or a drunkard, or a swindler — not even to eat with such a one. For what have I to do with judging an outsider? Do you not judge those who are within the church? But those who are outside, God judges. REMOVE THE WICKED MAN FROM AMONG YOURSELVES. **1 Corinthians 5:1 – 13 NASB**

We see a major difference between what Jesus speaks about in Matthew 18 and the situation Paul addresses in 1 Corinthians 5. The process in Matthew addresses a matter of private sin against another Christian. At issue in 1 Corinthians 5 is a sinful lifestyle that had turned into a public spectacle. Because it was public and ongoing, it communicated a disastrous message about Christ and his church to the city of Corinth and maybe even to the surrounding region. Even though there was no talk radio, television, or Internet in the first century, scandalous news could spread quickly.

It seems that Paul learned of this situation from others, not directly from the church (1 Corinthians 5:1). Since this was a public situation, it required a different, more immediate approach than following the three steps outlined in Matthew 18 and Titus 3. The expectation was that "the one who had done this deed would be removed from your midst" (1 Corinthians 5:2). Paul is saying that in a public situation like this, where there is gross immorality, the church must make a statement to the watching world that this is by no means the behavior of a true follower of Jesus Christ. *Good Point.*

## Pastoral Motivators to Confront Sin

Scripture is clear in telling us we *must* confront sin, but it doesn't say it is easy to do so. Other demands on our time can easily win out in our priorities. That's why we need "motivators" to help us remember our responsibility as a pastor to confront sin and lead our church in holiness. All of these motivators are biblically grounded, yet practical. Most of them are rooted in Paul's words to the Corinthian church, yet they are implied in many of the other passages referenced earlier.

### Confront Sin to Be Faithful to Scripture

Using a firm, loving tone in his letters, Paul writes that confrontation is necessary when we encounter Christians living in habitual, unrepentant sin. Quite often, confrontation does not lead to the results we desired; the actual results can be disappointing, even painful. So our greatest motivation is not how a person responds; we confront out of obedience to God's word, regardless of how someone responds. To be honest, every church discipline situation I've faced has been painful and difficult for our entire congregation. Yet our feelings should never trump what God clearly lays out in his word for us to do. We confront sin as shepherds of God's sheep because it means being faithful to Scripture.

## Confront Sin for the Church's Purity

Paul reminds the Corinthians that their indifference toward this gross immorality in the church is a result of their "boasting," which he says is "not good" (1 Corinthians 5:6 NASB). Then he gives an example to help the Corinthians understand why it is harmful to the purity of the church for this to remain unaddressed. He asks, "Do you not know that a little leaven leavens the whole lump of dough?" Paul is referring to the leaven in bread that makes it rise. All it takes is a little bit of leaven to cause the whole lump of dough to rise.

This cooking illustration reminds the church of the dangers of allowing sin to go on unaddressed. It only takes a little sin to poison the entire church. Paul is saying, "Remove the sin in your midst" before it spreads throughout the entire church as leaven does in dough. Church discipline is painful to execute, but pastors must carry it out for the purity and health of Christ's church.

## Confront Sin for the Sake of Christ's Name

Paul also writes that purity in the church is a reflection of the transformation that Jesus has brought to our lives. Paul uses the example of leavened bread and transitions to talking about the Passover celebration. Paul reminds his readers that Jesus Christ "our Passover also has been sacrificed" (1 Corinthians 5:7 NASB). Our lives are never free from the stain of sin. Yet Jesus lived the perfect life we cannot, died on the cross for our sins, and then rose from the dead to save us from our sins. This salvation changes our hearts to where we are now empowered to live differently. We are empowered by the Spirit of the living God that dwells in us as believers in Jesus to now live like Christ. We are no longer who we once were. Our sins have been paid for at the cross so we no longer have to walk in them. Paul's point is that the church displays Christ to the world by living as people transformed by the gospel.

So there is a problem when a church does not live out this transformation. When a church's members fail to walk in daily repentance of sin, a confusing and distorted picture of Jesus Christ is portrayed to the world. In the situation at Corinth, those who heard the report of sexual immorality in the church were getting a distorted picture of Christ and his bride. In their arrogance, the church at Corinth either missed what was being portrayed or, worse, didn't care that a distorted view of the gospel was on display. Paul makes this very point in verse 8: "Therefore let us celebrate the feast, not with old leaven, nor with the leaven of malice and wickedness, but with the unleavened bread of sincerity and truth" (1 Corinthians 5:8 NASB). The precious name of our Savior Jesus Christ is distorted before the world when pastors leave habitual, unrepentant sins unaddressed and fail to teach their congregations the need to live a Christlike life. We must heed the call to engage in discipline to honor the name of our Redeemer.

### Confront Sin for the Sake of One's Soul

Although there is a larger purpose in church discipline than just the individuals involved, the souls of those you confront matter greatly. Paul demonstrates his deep concern for the souls of those committing sin when he writes about delivering an unrepentant sinner to Satan for the destruction of his flesh, "so that his spirit may be saved in the day of the Lord Jesus" (1 Corinthians 5:5 NASB). This same concern comes across in the other three New Testament passages (Matthew 18; 2 Thessalonians 3; Titus 3). Though his words may sound harsh at first, Paul is speaking with a clear sense of eternal priorities in mind. He is reminding us that there are worse things than the pain of being removed from the formal fellowship of the church. Discipline that leads to loss of fellowship may have earthly, temporary consequences, but it may eventually lead a person to turn back to Christ. It is "tough love," a way of allowing time for the consequences of sin to penetrate the heart and hopefully lead a person to Christ.

Church discipline, in this sense, is a wake-up call to the one who lives carelessly and engages in sin like an unbeliever. Living this way communicates to others that a person is not truly converted. As such, they should be treated no longer as a member of the church but as an unbeliever. Of course, this does not mean treating them with hatred or rudeness. As a church, we minister to unbelievers in love and in the hope that the gospel will lead them to repentance. Although church discipline is painful and sometimes risky for the pastor who leads the church in this process, a pastor's ultimate concern must be for the souls of his people. Pastors must be willing to walk the difficult path of letting someone go, in the hope that someday a wayward, wandering sheep can be rescued.

## Conclusion

The irony of church discipline is that many people, including many Christians, wrongly assume that confronting sin is judgmental and unloving. Yet as we have seen, discipline is a loving act. Again, we need to keep the end in mind. How loving would it be to allow someone we love to continue in gross sinful behavior, allowing them to believe there are no consequences because they have a false sense of security? A person can think they are a Christian because they attend church or say an occasional prayer, but does their life reflect this confession? How tragic when a pastor knows of a habitual sin or lifestyle pattern and fears for a person's soul, yet says nothing! We do not want our sheep to meet Jesus one day and say to him, "Lord, I did this in your name, and I did that in your name, and I was in the leadership in your church ..."

only to have Jesus say to them, "I never knew you" (Matthew 7:23).

This, ultimately, is what lies behind the urgency of this call to action. God has ordained the use of discipline in the church as a means of saving souls and refining believers in their fight against sin. The process of church discipline also works to defend the purity and name of Jesus Christ to a watching world. Discipline is a loving act, done for the sake of souls. Though sinful decisions may reap earthly pain, our words of loving confrontation may be what lead people to their repentance, saving them on the last day (1 Corinthians 5:5).

Pastors are called to shepherd the souls of God's people, and there may be no more essential aspect of that calling than confronting a professing Christ follower in their habitual, unrepentant sin. If this is done in the manner and spirit prescribed by Scripture, there is no greater joy as a pastor than seeing a wandering sheep return home again. Sometimes, sadly, souls in our care go astray and don't return. Or we see no immediate, visible fruit from our efforts to confront sin. In those times, hang on to the biblical motivators and know that God is pleased and honored when we as undershepherds of the Chief Shepherd pursue wayward sheep in obedience to his word for the sake of his great name.

## Chapter 9

# Encourage the Weaker Sheep

> We urge you, brethren, admonish the unruly,
> encourage the fainthearted, help the weak, be patient
> with everyone. **1 Thessalonians 5:14 NASB**

Not long after a troubled couple walked through the doors of our church, I experienced one of the great joys of pastoral ministry. Neither one of them was a Christian, but they had come to me with a desire to get married. I explained I would need to meet with them for counseling, and they agreed to meet. After several months of meetings with my wife and me, this couple responded to the gospel and was baptized. A few months later, I married them in our church in a Christian wedding. Best of all, there was a captive audience of unbelievers in attendance who witnessed a picture of the gospel as they heard this couple speak their vows to one another. It was a special day, one I will always remember and treasure.

Discipling a new Christian believer can be challenging and messy. This couple was no different. They brought some devastating baggage into their new relationship with Christ, including several patterns from their past that made their marriage difficult. Thankfully, they were both teachable and eager to learn. Eventually, they had a child, and both the mom and the child had constant health issues, which added to the strain on the relationship.

Although the Spirit of God seemed to be at work in their lives, the dysfunctional patterns of sin and destructive living from the past made those first years of marriage and discipleship very difficult. Caring for them was taxing on our small congregation, so a number of people rotated in from time to time to help.

Only an omniscient God who knows all things can count the hours my wife and I logged caring for this family. So where is this couple today? Well, before I answer that question, let me ask another question: *Does it matter?* In other words, does their current membership status or level of involvement in the church determine whether or not our time and effort were worth it? In the world, we typically judge the success of our efforts based on the results they produce. This is the metric commonly used in the business world. It's how players and teams are judged in the world of professional sports. But I believe pastoral ministry is different. A pastor cannot simply measure his ministry by visible results because the results may not always be obvious on this side of eternity. The ministry of caring for and encouraging weaker brothers and sisters in our churches is one of those ministries where a pastor may not see immediate, obvious results. And yet pastors must still make room for this ministry. They must invest their time in the lives of people who can be draining and difficult. Why? Because it is *biblical*.

The aim of this chapter is to urge you to rethink models of ministry or advice you may have been given that suggested that as a pastor you should only invest your time and energy in people when it will lead to a positive result. Sometimes, pastors are tempted to ignore difficult people and challenging situations. They know it takes time to invest in helping a weaker brother or sister. It can be exhausting and frustrating at times. It will be a drain on a pastor's time and church resources in certain seasons. It may even cause a pastor to grow discouraged or question the power of God. You may even question on occasion whether or not a person is converted.

Paul calls these difficult people "the weak" (1 Thessalonians 5:14). And the weak are found in every church — those Christians who are easily swayed to turn away from their beliefs, who quickly grow discouraged, or who don't seem to experience much victory in their struggle against sin. As a result, they live with a tender conscience. They believe the gospel, show the presence of the Spirit in their lives, and listen to the instruction of God's word; yet they have a tough time internalizing and applying the truth of that word in their everyday lives because of personality, temperament, or past experience. In a conversation I once had with now-retired Baptist preacher Al Martin, he said, "Our job as pastors is to get as many people to heaven in the best condition possible." I like that because it reminds me that as pastors we aren't called to be the ones who make transformation possible. God does it, and he cares for the poor, weak, and needy among his people. As his shepherds, we simply care for the people God brings to us.

## The Heart of God toward the Weak

Weakness, pain, discouragement, and hopelessness all exist because of sin. These experiences are a direct result of the fall (Genesis 3). The good news is that God redeems the brokenness that results from sin through the person and work of Jesus Christ. Just as sinners receive undeserved mercy from a merciful God, we also receive God's compassion — his grace for the weak, needy, and afflicted. God's work of compassion began with his chosen people, Israel, and it continues today through the Spirit's work in the church.

### God's Care for the Weak in Israel

God's redemptive plan involves caring for the weak, poor, and afflicted among his own people. This tender care is evident throughout the psalms as the psalmists declare God's power to defend those unable to defend themselves:

God presides in the great assembly;
    he renders judgment among the "gods":
"How long will you defend the unjust
    and show partiality to the wicked?
Defend the weak and the fatherless;
    uphold the cause of the poor and the oppressed.
Rescue the weak and the needy;
    deliver them from the hand of the wicked."

**Psalm 82:1 – 4**

The prophets also speak of God's concern for the weak, feeble, and oppressed. Isaiah demonstrates God's promise of vindication for his redeemed people that is to come:

The desert and the parched land will be glad;
    the wilderness will rejoice and blossom.
Like the crocus, it will burst into bloom;
    it will rejoice greatly and shout for joy.
The glory of Lebanon will be given to it,
    the splendor of Carmel and Sharon;
they will see the glory of the LORD,
    the splendor of our God.
Strengthen the feeble hands,
    steady the knees that give way;
say to those with fearful hearts,
    "Be strong, do not fear;
your God will come,
    he will come with vengeance;
with divine retribution
    he will come to save you."

**Isaiah 35:1 – 4**

Isaiah reveals the promises God has made to his people, as well as the fate of Israel's enemies. God will one day come and judge with vengeance and divine retribution those who have turned against him and who have persecuted his people. He will give strength to the feeble, provision to the weak, and power to the fearful. These promises are given to lift the spirits of the weak and afflicted in Israel, as the entire nation anxiously awaits the coming King, the Messiah, who will usher in the fulfillment of these promises.

## Jesus' Compassion

As Jesus walked this earth, he revealed God's compassionate heart toward those who were weak, poor, and oppressed. Crowds of people with sicknesses, diseases, physical and mental weaknesses, and disheartened temperaments came to him for help. What was Jesus' response to them? He reflected compassion, patience, and hope for them. He did this in two ways.

First, Jesus' compassion and hope were visible through his *teaching ministry*. Consider what Jesus says in the Beatitudes, which are found at the beginning of the Sermon on the Mount. Consider the content and the intended audience in his opening words:

> Blessed are the poor in spirit,
> for theirs is the kingdom of heaven.
> Blessed are those who mourn,
> for they will be comforted.
> Blessed are the meek,
> for they will inherit the earth.
> Blessed are those who hunger and thirst for righteousness,
> for they will be filled.
> Blessed are the merciful,
> for they will be shown mercy.
> Blessed are the pure in heart,
> for they will see God.
> Blessed are the peacemakers,
> for they will be called children of God.

> Blessed are those who are persecuted because of righ-
> teousness,
>     for theirs is the kingdom of heaven.
>
> **Matthew 5:1–10**

Jesus begins his foundational teaching on the kingdom of God by addressing the poor, the mournful, the meek, the righteous, the merciful, the pure, the peacemakers, and the persecuted. Jesus turns upside down the common thought of his day about the kingdom of God. He doesn't exalt the powerful and the influential; he speaks about the poor and the meek as the ones who will inherit the kingdom. Paul would later write that we are strong when we are at our weakest (2 Corinthians 12:10). In the kingdom, the first will be last, and the last first (Matthew 19:30). And those who wish to be first must be a slave, a servant to all (Mark 10:44). Jesus taught that the weak have a significant place in the kingdom of God.

Second, Jesus' compassion and hope were visible through his *interactions with the sick, lame, and blind.* Matthew gives a striking summation of Jesus' care for those who are weak and afflicted:

> Jesus left there and went along the Sea of Galilee.
> Then he went up on a mountainside and sat down.
> Great crowds came to him, bringing the lame, the
> blind, the crippled, the mute and many others, and laid
> them at his feet; and he healed them. The people were
> amazed when they saw the mute speaking, the crippled
> made well, the lame walking and the blind seeing. And
> they praised the God of Israel.          **Matthew 15:29–31**

Jesus reached out to those who had been ostracized from society and had lost hope. He not only restored their strength through physical healing, but he gave them hope in this life, as well as for the life to come. The cross and resurrection sealed that hope, and the compassion of Jesus toward the weak becomes the foundation for the apostles' ministry toward others. We see evidence of this in the New Testament and how they instruct Christ's followers in his church.

## The Apostles' Call

The apostles continued the mercy ministry of Jesus, and we read about this throughout the book of Acts. The leaders of the early church continued to heal the lame, sick, and blind. They demonstrated to all the continuing power of the Holy Spirit in their care of the weak and afflicted. The apostle Paul also gave specific instructions that the church should help the weak and be patient with those who are slow to learn and change: "We urge you, brethren, admonish the unruly, encourage the fainthearted, help the weak, be patient with everyone. See that no one repays another with evil for evil, but always seek after that which is good for one another and for all people" (1 Thessalonians 5:14–15 NASB).

Paul is writing to the church in Thessalonica, where there is the looming presence of false teachers trying to lead the faithful astray. Believers who were fainthearted and weak were at particular risk, which is why Paul urges the Christians in that church to pay particular attention to those most susceptible to the wolves in sheep's clothing. This includes the unruly, the fainthearted, and the weak.

In addition, the church faced frequent disagreements among members that included arguments about specific beliefs or practices. Some of these were matters of conscience, "disputable matters," as Paul puts it (Romans 14:1). Unfortunately, those in the church who were weak in faith and disposition had the potential to have their faith damaged or destroyed by these issues. So Paul writes this instruction:

> Accept the one whose faith is weak, without quarreling over disputable matters. One person's faith allows them to eat anything, but another, whose faith is weak, eats only vegetables. The one who eats

> everything must not treat with contempt the one who
> does not, and the one who does not eat everything
> must not judge the one who does, for God has accepted
> them.
> **Romans 14:1 – 3**

Paul is aware that this issue of conscience had become a source of great division among the Corinthian church, and he spends three chapters (1 Corinthians 8 – 10) addressing the matter. In that case, the question was whether meat sacrificed to an idol could be eaten. Paul carefully walks through the issue, urging the Christians in Corinth to exercise Christian liberty, yet not as an opportunity to flaunt their freedom in Christ, but always with the motive of loving and caring for those who disagree with them — the weaker brother or sister.

> However not all men have this knowledge; but
> some, being accustomed to the idol until now, eat food
> as if it were sacrificed to an idol; and their conscience
> being weak is defiled. But food will not commend us
> to God; we are neither the worse if we do not eat, nor
> the better if we do eat. But take care that this liberty
> of yours does not somehow become a stumbling
> block to the weak. For if someone sees you, who have
> knowledge, dining in an idol's temple, will not his
> conscience, if he is weak, be strengthened to eat things
> sacrificed to idols? For through your knowledge he who
> is weak is ruined, the brother for whose sake Christ died.
> And so, by sinning against the brethren and wounding
> their conscience when it is weak, you sin against Christ.
> Therefore, if food causes my brother to stumble, I will
> never eat meat again, so that I will not cause my brother
> to stumble.
> **1 Corinthians 8:7 – 13 NASB**

Paul reminds the Corinthians that the goal is not to prove oneself right at the expense of others. It is to encourage those who are weaker in the faith, both to demonstrate the love of Christ to them and to display the unifying power of the gospel to a watching world. Showing care, compassion, and concern for the weak in the congregation is one of the ways we make Christ's compassion known to others.

## Finding Balance

The apostles gave specific instructions to encourage the fainthearted and consider the weaker brother or sister, but how is this accomplished? As we acknowledged earlier, this type of ministry is often time-consuming and requires patience and wisdom. It can be taxing on pastors and on the entire church as well. So how do you labor in this and not grow dispirited, frustrated, and impatient? I think it is helpful to approach pastoral ministry with weaker brothers or sisters, with "problem people," by thinking through four characteristics of this ministry. We must have patience, hope, help from others, and compassion for those in need.

### Encourage with Patience

The progress of sanctification is typically slow, and shepherding the soul of weaker brothers or sisters requires a lot of time and effort. You'll grow frustrated and have the same conversations over and over. You will feel like your brother or sister in Christ is losing ground in their struggle. Patience is an invaluable asset in these situations.

When a pastor senses he is growing frustrated with a weaker person or is growing impatient over the lack of change and growth, it's helpful to take a step back and consider this question: How does my timeline for change contrast with God's timeline? The truth is that we are never guaranteed a certain rate of growth that is the same for every individual. Each person is unique, facing different challenges in the fight against sin. The most empowered and victorious Christian still battles sin, the flesh, and the Devil every day in this fallen world. And those who are fainthearted and weak face this battle as well, often with fewer weapons at their disposal.

As a pastor, you cannot assume your own experience or the limited experience you've had with others will hold true for each and every individual. A pastor who embraces this spiritual reality and continues to trust in God's timing will be a more patient pastor. Spend time reflecting on the patience God shows toward you and your own sins and shortcomings. How wonderful that God is slow to anger and abounding in steadfast love, even when we are most undeserving of it! Remembering the patience of our kind God toward us will help to cultivate patience toward others.

*Great Point!*

## Encourage with Hope

It's normal to get discouraged when we deal with someone who keeps making the same mistakes and committing the same sins over and over again. I can still recall the despair I felt when I was called back multiple times to the home of a couple in our church. They were constantly fighting and bickering, typically around the time I was getting ready for bed. I would go to their home and attempt to bring peace into the situation. Things would calm down, but then next month, as I was getting ready for bed, the phone would ring again. And again next month. Then, one month, they ended up at my front door. But nothing seemed to change.

The repetition and the lack of change or progress in breaking these painful patterns almost broke me! The power of ingrained behavioral patterns of sin can lead even the most upbeat and optimistic pastor to despair. In our discouragement, we can begin to doubt the power of God. Our optimism and faith in God begin to fade as we see little to no result, even after years of ministry.

The gospel gives us hope, even when we don't see immediate change. When we take our eyes off the gospel and forget its power, we will naturally begin to lose hope. But the gospel *is enough* to give us hope, even in the most despairing of circumstances. It is a message of resurrection from death to life. It is a promise of freedom for those enslaved. It is a promise of a future when everything is made new, even as the world around us never seems to change.

This doesn't mean we will no longer face great suffering and hardship in this world. The hope of Christ gives us the assurance that no situation or relationship is too difficult and hopeless for Jesus. In his work on the cross, Jesus brought forgiveness for our sins and delivered us from the wrath of God. We have been rescued from eternal punishment.

Do we still believe Jesus is too weak to heal a marriage? Is Jesus unable to overcome a drug addiction in a new convert? Is Jesus not powerful enough to help a man overcome his ensnarement to pornography?

We have been eternally adopted as children of God. Jesus has been raised from death to life, and he will one day raise us to enjoy new bodies like his. The gospel of Jesus Christ and the power of the Holy Spirit that dwells in every follower of Jesus give us hope. Real hope, not just wishful thinking. When we find ourselves losing hope or despairing, this can be God's way of refining our faith, helping us see where we have been relying on our abilities and efforts or the efforts of the person we are helping rather than on the Holy Spirit. God's timing is not ours, nor are his ways our ways.

You *can* have hope that people will overcome their sins, but don't place your hope in your abilities or efforts. Persevere in faith by relying on God's promises; faithfully and patiently continue to do the work of caring and ministering for those in need. Pastors, as you care for the fainthearted in your flock, be hopeful and have faith in the Spirit, who is always at work.

### Encourage with Help from Others

Pastors are not to lose heart or allow discouragement to set in, and yet the reality is that our ministry is taxing and demanding. Caring for those who are weak requires a corporate effort. Many people need to be involved. A pastor needs to invite others into these situations and allow them to serve. This can be hard for pastors to do for several reasons. Some pastors deceive themselves into thinking they are the only ones able to minister — or the one being ministered to believes only the pastor can help. I've had pastors say to me, "I *have* to meet with [so and so] because they will only meet with me. I'm the only one who knows all the details of their situation." One of the worst things you can do in these situations is assume you are the only one able to offer care. Allow others to help! And be humble enough to recognize that the perspectives and experiences others bring are indispensable.

In our church, on occasion a weaker brother was assigned to a mature brother, who would then disciple him for a time. In some cases, after approximately six months we'd see the drain on the person doing the discipling and arrange for another brother to take over. Six months later, we shifted again, and we've found that these shifts have great benefit for the man in need. Each person brings a unique perspective and set of life experiences. One man approached the struggles this brother was having differently than another and was able to reach this brother in unique ways. Eventually, this struggling brother began to grow in the Lord as a result of all these investments, and he gradually became less taxing on those investing in him. Pastors do a disservice to those in need when they refuse to involve others and ask for their help.

## Encourage with Compassion

When frustration sets in as effort after effort bears no fruit, many pastors conclude that this is God's way of saying, "Give up; move on." We need to be cautious in thinking this way, because our frustration may be less an accurate assessment of what God is saying or not saying and more likely God's way of revealing our lack of compassion. Compassion is most clearly displayed in our care in those moments when we are frustrated and ready to give up—but then we don't. We press on. We try again. We speak the same encouraging words we've spoken many times before in the anticipation that the Spirit of God will one day allow them to stick. *W.7h Cody*

Compassion is a gift from the Lord, and it can be one of a pastor's greatest assets. How do we find that compassion? How do we receive it? Similar to hope and patience, we must remember and meditate on the compassion Jesus has shown us. Would God be justified if he got frustrated with you? And yet we know he meets us, not in anger, guilt, and shame, but with an ever-flowing river of grace that flows from the foot of the cross. God is merciful to us in our weakness, and we are to show our flock that same compassion as shepherds. We treat them as the Chief Shepherd has treated us. In fact, the mercy and compassion we show to our family and flock can be a tool the Spirit uses to help others receive God's grace in their own lives.

## Conclusion

I wish the story I shared earlier in this chapter had a happy ending. Unfortunately, the couple's struggles continued, and the husband eventually abandoned both his family and his faith and was disciplined out of the church. We continued our appeal to him to repent and return, but at this point he has refused to change. His wife, however, despite being abandoned by her husband and left alone to find a job and care for her daughter, has shown inspiring levels of faith in God through this trial. It has been very difficult for her. She constantly struggles financially and wonders how her monthly needs will be met. She's had many nights when she has had to try to answer the painful questions from her angry and confused daughter.

It has been encouraging to see this young woman flourish in so many ways in her growth in Christ throughout these trials, and I've been blessed to see the church rally around her as they've extended sacrificial care and provision to her and her daughter. Although we cannot understand all that God is doing in these painful events, it is clear he is at work to mature the weaker sheep, equip the local church, and bring great glory to Christ and the power of the gospel at work in his people.

Caring for and encouraging a weaker brother or sister is the calling of all Christians in the local church. Pastors bear the responsibility to train and equip others to do this work, since it requires a corporate effort. Look for members who are mature, stable, and gifted enough to engage in this ministry, because it is not easy! Recognize this task as a significant priority for your ministry and lead by your example, showing your church members how to live out the compassion and mercy that Christ has shown to you. This balance is powerfully captured by the sixteenth-century pastor Martin Bucer. After explaining how to encourage and strengthen the fainthearted in the local church, Bucer writes these words:

> This is how the weak and ailing sheep of Christ are to be strengthened and comforted, and this is to be done by all Christians. For since Christ lives in all his members, he will also exercise this pastoral work of his in all. But because the carers of souls are specially ordained for this purpose, it is fitting that they should also pursue this work of the care of souls before any other, and carry it out most faithfully. Rulers are to see that the churches are provided with carers of souls who are keen and zealous in this work, and perform this work in all weak and foolish sheep, and are to encourage them with all faithfulness, thus also exercising for their part their ministry to Christ the Chief Shepherd in this work of helping and strengthening the sick and ailing sheep. So this, as we have said, is all directed at seeing that through the holy gospel of Christ people are well instructed and reminded to seek everything in Christ our Lord alone, and be satisfied with all things in him.[24]

Pastors who make this difficult but important aspect of

shepherding souls a priority in their ministries and "carry it out most faithfully" will see not just the weaker brothers and sisters in their midst encouraged and cared for, but also a local church more equipped to carry out the commands of Christ. These pastors and their congregations will likely do so with more compassion, empathy, and hope in their souls than would be present otherwise.

Chapter 10

# Identify and Train Leaders

> You then, my son, be strong in the grace that is in Christ Jesus. And the things you have heard me say in the presence of many witnesses entrust to reliable people who will also be qualified to teach others.
>
> **2 Timothy 2:1–2**

The great nineteenth-century evangelist George Whitefield summarized well the reason so many churches in his day were spiritually dead.* He writes, "The reason why congregations have been so dead is, because they have dead men preaching to them."[25] There are churches that have dead men (spiritually) preaching to them, prideful men guiding them, and greedy men abusing them. There are countless stories of unfaithful shepherds who harm the sheep. Stories abound of pastors abusing their position to embezzle money or to pursue sexually a vulnerable married woman in their congregation. It is a beautiful sight to see Christ's church led by biblically called, qualified men; it is equally tragic to watch wolves in sheep's clothing infiltrate the church and ravish Christ's people. The only remedy is identifying and training leaders within the local church—a task that must be a top priority for the pastor.

---

*This chapter summarizes content originally published in Brian Croft, *Prepare Them to Shepherd* (Grand Rapids: Zondervan, 2014).

Pastors make two common mistakes when identifying and training leaders. The first mistake is thinking this responsibility falls on those outside the local church. Seminaries, Bible colleges, mission organizations, and other parachurch ministries have largely taken the reins when it comes to this task. But the Bible gives a different understanding. When Paul and Barnabas were about to be sent on their first missionary journey, it was the church in Antioch that prayed, laid hands on them, and sent them out (Acts 13:1 – 3). Ministries outside the local church have been very useful in accomplishing God's work in the world, but according to the Scriptures, these ministries are not responsible to identify and train pastors and other leaders. The local church bears that burden — more specifically, pastors and church leaders.

The second mistake is to conclude that a person is called to be a leader in a church simply because they sense an inward desire to do so (internal calling). Sadly, many churches today place leaders in important positions on the basis of nothing more than an individual's sense — his own subjective perception — of their *internal* calling. If a man has the desire to do the work of the ministry and seems gifted, the church assumes he is called. To be sure, a man's own assessment is important; nonetheless, the church cannot rely on a subjective assessment or an unfalsifiable feeling in the man himself. They need a tangible process that tests a man's qualifications for ministry against those laid out in Scripture. Paul writes to Timothy and states clearly that a person has certain qualifications to meet to be a leader in the church (1 Timothy 3:1 – 13), and men should be evaluated and affirmed as reliable before being entrusted with this role (2 Timothy 2:2).

## Identify Biblically Qualified Leaders

The Bible gives several clear and specific qualifications that a church leader should possess. They do not need to have a savvy business mind or a winsome personality. Instead, these qualifications are rooted in their calling as shepherds who care for God's people. Although there are two main offices in the New Testament church, pastor (sometimes called "elder" or "overseer" in the New Testament) and deacon, the focus of this chapter will be on the qualifications of pastors—those who are called to lead and shepherd Christ's church. The primary passage that highlights the detailed qualifications of a pastor of God's people in the local church is found in 1 Timothy 3:1–7. Saints of past and present have seen three broad qualifications for a pastor based on this passage.[26]

## 1. One Who Is Transformed by the Gospel

A man who senses an internal call to enter the sacred office of a minister of the gospel must first be transformed by the gospel. The gospel is the message of salvation from sin and from God's wrath. It declares that a sinner receives salvation by grace through repentance of sin and through faith in the person and work of Jesus Christ. It may seem obvious that a man entering the ministry should have saving faith in Christ. Yet, time after time, the issue of unconverted pastors has been a legitimate concern. In the seventeenth century, for example, Richard Baxter began his celebrated book *The Reformed Pastor* this way:

> Take heed to yourselves, lest you be void of that saving grace of God which you offer to others, and be strangers to the effectual working of that gospel which you preach; and lest, while you proclaim to the world the necessity of a Savior, your own hearts should neglect him and you should miss of an interest in him and his saving benefits. Take heed to yourselves, lest you perish, while you call upon others to take heed of perishing; and lest you famish yourselves while you prepare food for them ... Many have warned others that they come not to that place of torment, while yet they hastened to it themselves; many a preacher is now in hell, who hath a hundred times called upon his hearers to use the utmost care and diligence to escape it.[27]

Baxter's warning should continue to resonate with us in the

twenty-first century. Much is at stake if local churches neglect the importance of carefully evaluating candidates for pastoral ministry. If a man is still in darkness, enslaved to sin, and living in rebellion against God, he should not be placed in a position where he is entrusted with the gospel and the responsibility of shepherding redeemed souls.

## 2. One Who Earnestly Desires the Work

The apostle Paul instructs his young protégé, "Here is a trustworthy saying: Whoever aspires to be an overseer [pastor] desires a noble task" (1 Timothy 3:1). The great nineteenth-century Baptist preacher Charles Spurgeon lectured young men preparing for the ministry: "The first sign of the heavenly calling is an intense, all-absorbing desire for the work."[28] There should be a strong, unquenchable desire in a man to do the work of a pastor. He should have a desire to preach God's word, shepherd God's people, evangelize the lost, disciple the spiritually immature, and serve the local church.

Spurgeon suggests this divine aspiration can be known through a desire to do nothing else:

> If any student in this room could be content to be a newspaper editor, or a grocer, or a farmer, or a doctor, or a lawyer, or a senator, or a king, in the name of heaven and earth, let him go his way; he is not the man in whom dwells the Spirit of God in its fullness, for a man so filled with God would utterly weary of any pursuit but that for which his inmost soul pants. If on the other hand, you can say that for all the wealth of both the Indies you could not and dare not espouse any other calling so as to be put aside from preaching the gospel of Jesus Christ, then depend upon it, if other things be equally satisfactory, you have the signs of this apostleship. We must feel that woe is unto us if we preach not the gospel; the word of God must be unto us as fire in our bones, otherwise, if we undertake the ministry, we shall be unhappy in it, shall be unable to bear the self-denials

incident to it, and shall be of little service to those among whom we minister.[29]

Why is an unquenchable longing for this work required? Because the work of ministry is not for the faint of heart. It is a work fraught with struggles, challenges, discouragements, pressures, and spiritual battles that can cripple the strongest of men who have only an "ordinary" desire for the work. It should be a desire that cannot be stolen when your brother betrays you, weakened when your job is threatened, or quenched when physical, mental, and emotional fatigue firmly take root. A Christian man who has an "irresistible, overwhelming craving and raging thirst"[30] for this fine work should enter this work.

There must also be earnestness to this desire. The nineteenth-century English minister John Angell James reminds us of how a pastor cultivates it:

> Every minister can be an earnest minister if he so wills: he is earnest when any thing in which he has a deep interest is at stake. Let his house be on fire, or his health or life be in danger, or his wife or child be in peril, or some means of greatly augmenting his property be thrown in his way, and what intensity of emotion and vehemence of action will be excited in him! He needs but the pressure upon his conscience of the interests of immortal souls; he needs but a heart so constrained by the love of Christ, as to be borne away by the force and impetuosity of that hallowed passion; he needs but a longing desire to be wise in winning men to Jesus; he needs, in fine, but a heart fully set to accomplish the ends and objects of his office, to possess that high and noble quality of soul which it is the object of this work to recommend.[31]

A strong desire for the work of the ministry does not always mean an earnestness will accompany it. A man should honestly examine whether he has the earnestness of that strong desire before setting his hand to pursue this work.

### 3. One Who Possesses Biblical Character

Many faithful, godly men throughout the ages have displayed Christ in their character and have modeled sacrificial service to his church. Yet not all have been called to the work of pastor/elder. Paul gives Timothy a separate list of qualifications for this office (1 Timothy 3:1–7) that is distinct from that of deacons (verses 8–13). This list demonstrates that there is a unique calling and work that a pastor is set apart to do. These qualifications provide a way for others to evaluate externally and objectively a man who claims to have a desire for this work. Paul's list of qualifications for the office of pastor can be divided into five categories:

### 1. One Who Is Able to Teach

The ability to teach (1 Timothy 3:2) is the primary qualification that sets apart the work of a pastor from that of all others in the church. This qualification refers to more than just a desire to teach; it involves having the skill to teach God's word faithfully, accurately, and effectively. Paul confirms this in his second letter to Timothy, when he writes that God has entrusted these men to guard the gospel — "the good deposit . . . with the help of the Holy Spirit who lives in us" (2 Timothy 1:14).

This requirement of being able to teach should also be understood in light of what James writes about teachers. James warns that those who teach in the church "will be judged more strictly" (James 3:1). Those who have been gifted by God for this task should do so humbly, clearly, passionately, and faithfully. The call to teach involves preaching the word (2 Timothy 4:2), no matter the cost, seizing every opportunity to make the gospel clear by presenting the treasure and value of Christ, calling people to repent and believe, and then trusting in the power of the Holy Spirit to transform hearts and minds. The ability to instruct God's people with his word is referred to as correcting, rebuking, and encouraging (2 Timothy 4:2), and it should define gospel ministry, both public and private. The Baptist minister Roger

Ellsworth has rightly observed, "Fail here and you would have failed in your central task."[32]

## 2. One Who Has a Blameless Reputation

Paul's command that a pastor "is to be above reproach" (1 Timothy 3:2) emphasizes that a pastor should not just flee from evil but should seek to avoid even the appearance of evil. For example, it's difficult to accuse a pastor of having an affair if it is widely known that he will not be alone in a room with another woman (with the exception of his wife, of course). The qualification of having a blameless reputation means a pastor should seek to live in a way that avoids accusations. He should seek to live a consistent, godly life and cultivate a good reputation among all people. The fact that he is not in bondage to any substance but is self-controlled affirms this reputation, which seems to be why Paul also mentions he should not be "given to drunkenness" (1 Timothy 3:3).

Having a blameless reputation also involves having a "good reputation with outsiders, so that he will not fall into disgrace and into the devil's trap" (1 Timothy 3:7). This does not mean backing down from the truth or trying to compromise with the world; it means living in a way that demonstrates God's love and compassion for the lost — that "they may see your good deeds and glorify God on the day he visits us" (1 Peter 2:12).

## 3. One Who Faithfully Manages His Family

A third qualification for the call to be a pastor is to be "faithful to his wife" (1 Timothy 3:2). This phrase is commonly misunderstood to mean a pastor must be married and cannot be single, but Paul here isn't referring to marital status but rather to faithfulness — that a married man is committed and faithful to his one wife. A pastor's leadership in the home is shown by the depth of his love for his wife and his commitment to living sacrificially, "just as Christ loved the church and gave himself up for her"

(Ephesians 5:25). All Christian husbands are commanded to love their wives in this way, but a pastor is called to model this for his people.

This qualification reflects Paul's additional instructions to Timothy that a woman is not to "assume authority over a man" (1 Timothy 2:12). Just as men are to lead their families, God's design is for the men to lead the church. This principle also applies to children living in a pastor's home. A pastor is to shepherd, teach, care, and manage his children faithfully (1 Timothy 3:4). This expectation does not require a pastor to have children or that his children must necessarily be converted. It means a pastor's children must respect his authority as the God-appointed head and leader of the family. Why does this matter? Paul gives a profound reason: "If anyone does not know how to manage his own family, how can he take care of God's church?" (1 Timothy 3:5).

Along with managing his household, a pastor should be warm and welcoming toward outsiders and visitors to his home. He should be "hospitable" (1 Timothy 3:2). Most people only think of this as welcoming people into one's home, which is certainly true, but hospitality more generally speaks of our disposition and attitude toward strangers. It's not difficult to be hospitable to people you know and love, but not many of us are hospitable to strangers we don't know. Paul tells us a pastor should model a willingness to care for others—even those he does not know. He also implies that he should guide his household to embrace this as a calling for the entire family.

### 4. One Who Has a Godly Character

Most of the characteristics Paul lists can be placed in the general category of godly character. Paul tells us a pastor is to be "temperate, self-controlled, respectable" (1 Timothy 3:2), as well as "gentle, not quarrelsome" (verse 3). All of these qualities speak of the inward transformation of the gospel and of how Christ is reflected in a person who is kind, compassionate, self-controlled in words and deeds, honorable, humble, and full of discernment and wisdom. It is difficult to overstate the importance of this requirement for leadership and ministry. Basil Manly Jr. writes this:

> It need scarcely be said that *piety* is essential. No amount of talent, no extent of education, no apparent brilliancy of fervor, should ever be allowed to gain admission into the ministry for one whose piety there is a reason to doubt, or who has not a more than ordinary active and consistent holiness. A Christless minister is as horribly out of place as a ghastly skeleton in the pulpit, bearing a torch in his hand.[33]

It is no accident that most of Paul's qualifications fall into this category of godly character. Those who desire the work of pastoral ministry should labor diligently to grow in these qualities, knowing it is the grace of God and the transforming power of the gospel that empower their growth.

### 5. One Who Possesses Spiritual Maturity

Many of these qualities also point to the requirement of spiritual maturity, but two qualities in particular indicate its necessity. First, Paul tells us a pastor is to be "not a lover of money" (1 Timothy 3:3). His primary responsibility is to preach and teach the word of God and sacrificially care for his people, not to seek financial gain for himself. Assessing if a person is free from the love of money is not about how much money a pastor has or what his annual salary is; it is about what the pastor does with his money. Loving money speaks to a desire to have more and more of it. A pastor should be compensated for the work he does, but a man should not enter the ministry out of a desire for personal material gain.

Second, as a spiritual leader and doctrinal gatekeeper of the church, a pastor cannot be "a recent convert" (1 Timothy 3:6). A spiritually immature person should not enter this work. This makes sense for obvious reasons, but in the text Paul gives a specific one: "he may become conceited and fall under the same judgment as the devil." An immature believer can easily get caught up in the power of the position instead of seeing the office as sacrificial service to God and his people. Pursuing pastoral ministry also places a man on the front lines of spiritual attack from the enemy, which seems to be one of the several reasons the New Testament calls for a plurality of godly, spiritually mature pastors/elders in a local church. Having multiple pastors and elders allows for greater accountability and fellowship, while also benefiting the church with their accumulated wisdom (Acts 20:28; Titus 1:5; 1 Peter 5:1).

## Training and Identifying Leaders

We should never assume that just because someone is smart and can talk as if they know how something is done, they actually know how to do it. A person can get excited about skydiving because they read a book about it, but that person is no more prepared to skydive than a person is ready to preach because they heard a good sermon. Applying what we have learned about ministry preparation to our own local church context is essential. Wisdom is gained through trial and error, as we put this imperative into practice.

The passage that tells of the sending of Paul and Barnabas (Acts 13:1–3) is a snapshot of a moment in a particular church and a particular culture. It is helpful to consider it a template to identify and train leaders. Even so, we need to remember that the Bible does not describe a detailed, line-by-line procedure for identifying and training those who feel called to be pastors and church leaders. Having said this, most of the following suggestions are the result of efforts I have made in our own local church. We have found four progressive steps to be beneficial as we seek to identify and train leaders for the local church.

## *Test*

Paul tells the Ephesian church that God gives some men to the church who are apostles, prophets, evangelists, and pastors and teachers for the equipping and building up the church (Ephesians 4:11–12). The best way to find these men in your own local church context is to test those who sense an internal calling to this work. To test someone involves placing them in a variety of real-life circumstances and observing how they handle them. The best way to test men for the office of pastor is to evaluate them in life circumstances as they do the work of a pastor, bearing in mind the qualifications mapped out in Scripture (1 Timothy 3:1–7; Titus 1:5–9). Over time, we can begin to determine whether a young man desiring this work is truly called, especially as his gifts to preach and teach are tested. This testing should occur visibly before the congregation.

For example, we have twelve different men preach on a different psalm on Sunday evenings every summer. These men want to test their gifts to preach. It is a way for the church body to consider their giftedness while also giving them an opportunity to serve our church. We encourage members to approach each individual after the service to give specific comments of encouragement and critique in a loving, helpful way. In addition, a mandatory service review is held after the Sunday evening service in which the pastors and a few other men involved in testing their gifts speak kindly and truthfully into this brother's life and give feedback about the sermon. Encouragement is given, corrections are made, and suggestions are submitted so he can improve for the next opportunity.

These brothers are also tested when they visit church members' homes. They go to offer care for an individual member, and a pastor observes them or gathers feedback from others to determine how well they are serving and what fruit comes as a result. We will pay attention to how self-controlled, hospitable, gentle, peaceful, above reproach, and respectable they are, which are all qualities Paul highlights (1 Timothy 3:1–7; Titus 1:5–9). When a brother who wants to do the work of a shepherd cares for a dying saint in the hospital who needs a word of comfort, the ground of testing is significantly plowed. It is a great encouragement to watch a young man courageously face this testing period and see his pastor's heart emerge.

I once challenged a young man to visit a homebound member who, though he was a sweet and kind man, was hard to understand when he spoke and could not read or write. Because this man was difficult to engage at times, I knew this would be a good testing ground for a young aspiring shepherd. Not only did this young man care well for this elderly saint; he also chose to visit him often, just to spend time with him. Knowing the man couldn't read, this young man was able to discern his unique need and respond by bringing him audiotapes of the Bible and sermons preached at our church. The testing process surely contains risks, but when challenges are met by men testing their gifts, and those gifts emerge, there is great satisfaction. The risks prove to be worth it.

In God's kind providence, every portion of an individual's testing works for the good of the local church as a whole. When a brother preaches, he is feeding God's people through his labor in the word. When a brother disciples another brother, he is helping him mature and grow in his faith in Christ. When a brother visits a homebound church member or a member in the hospital, he is caring for the soul of that member and ultimately serving the pastors and church in his efforts. As they serve the church in the midst of this testing, they are beginning to learn the daily labors of ministry that cannot be learned from reading books or taking classes. This is the start of hands-on training for the ministry.

## Train

Testing that is done more frequently and intentionally becomes training. By this time, the pastors of the church have identified to some degree gifts in an individual (according to 1 Timothy 3:1–7) that must be deliberately developed. At this point, a brother begins to play a more active role in church leadership: regularly teaching classes, leading services, or preaching on Sunday evenings for a month. The pastors now trust them enough to send them to the hospitals on their own and expose them more regularly to the decisions and directions of the church. They may begin to evaluate the sermons and the services every week. In all these things, they are being trained for ministry, and church members continue to be served, encouraged, and cared for through their efforts.

At a recent commissioning service for missionaries of our congregation, I exhorted a family who had been through this stage of the process:

> You, _____ [husband and wife], have been in many of
> our homes and us in yours. We have had the joy of fellowship
> with you. You have served our church in so many ways. You,
> _____ [wife], have cared for our children as you have faith-
> fully cared for your own. You modeled a Christlike attitude
> through a very difficult family schedule. You, _____ [hus-
> band], have faithfully preached and taught God's word to us.
> You have helped several people spiritually grow through your
> discipleship efforts. You, _____ [husband], have helped
> lead our public gatherings and have used your pastoral experi-
> ence to help the pastors think through some difficult issues.
> However, as we fellowshipped together and served with you
> both, something else was happening—you were being tested
> and trained before our eyes for the work to which you felt called.
> By God's grace, he has allowed our church the joy of Christian
> fellowship with you through that time to put us in a place to
> affirm you.

The specific details of the training depend on the gifts of the individual and the ministry they are called to. An aspiring pastor may spend more time doing soul care and developing his preaching, while an aspiring missionary may be more focused on evangelism and developing leaders. The key is that the training is centered within the local church, is led by the pastors, and is ministry to members of the church. Ultimately, this is what allows a local church as a whole to be in a position where they can affirm a man's gifts and calling.

## Affirm

After the pastors and leaders have taken adequate time to test and train a brother pursuing the ministry, the time comes when they must decide to either affirm him or not affirm him. After prayer and thoughtful discussion, if the pastors feel a brother demonstrates evidence of internal and external calling, we recommend him to the congregation for a formal time of evaluation. Because much of his testing and training has been visibly carried out with the people of the church, they should be informed enough to make their own decision. Often, we will have fruitful discussions in our members' meetings, and if no concerns are raised, the church comes back after a month of praying to vote to affirm the call.

This affirmation can come in several ways. It may be an affirmation for a brother to serve as an assistant pastor in our church. It may be an affirmation for them to pursue a ministry position at another local church. It may be a vote to affirm a couple who desires to enter the mission field. It may be to affirm someone to plant a church elsewhere in the city. Regardless of specific details, the decision to ordain a brother as a pastor or missionary should involve a public affirmation, which serves as a sign that they have the full support of our local church.

Here is an excerpt of a public statement I once made to our church about a family that was pursuing missionary work. The statement reveals the kind of scrutiny we use when evaluating those who sense an internal calling:

> I have had one-on-one meetings with this couple to discuss their marriage, family, educational challenges, and struggles with sin. The pastors have discussed their situation on numerous

occasions. We have had several public discussions about this family at our members' meetings. Yet, they still sit here desiring our affirmation, because in all those discussions, we as a church have felt convinced, though the road they face will be hard, that this is the work the Lord has for them.

Such statements are designed to remind the congregation that we have gone through a carefully planned identifying and training process to get to this point. It also indicates the time has come to affirm the call. Regardless of the structure of your polity, every congregation should eventually come to a point of affirmation where the whole church plays a role. This point is rightfully made by Martin Bucer in his masterful pastoral theology written in the early sixteenth century: "It is necessary to have the consensus of the whole church, because ministers are not only to be blameless in the eyes of the Lord's people, but also well trusted and loved by them."[34] Once an individual has been tested, trained, and affirmed by the leaders and congregation, we are ready to do what God has called us to do, namely, send them out!

### Send

Sending someone out from the church can be a complicated and involved process. They may be pursuing a pastorate or working in the mission field or simply taking a step to pursue theological education. In each case, we are committing to do a number of things as we send them:

- Pray regularly for them
- Share wisdom and pastoral oversight regarding where they should go
- Be in regular contact while they are gone or serving on the field
- Support them financially, when necessary—especially if the individual or family is going to a mission field without funding from a particular organization

- Ensure ongoing pastoral oversight and encouragement to become involved in a local church for individuals pursuing theological education

Sending is never the end of the process; it is the start of a new commitment by a local church to give our blessing and support to those who have been tested, trained, affirmed, and sent out.

Several years ago, we sent a dear missionary couple with this new commitment in mind. We regularly prayed for them as a church. The pastors were in regular contact to give counsel and care from afar. I was directly involved in their care for their first four-year term on the field, which at times involved late-night Skype sessions as they faced crisis moments when little help on the field was available. They recently returned for a one-year furlough and were warmly received into our fellowship. Those of us who sent them four years before were eager to care for them and meet their needs for fellowship, soul care, and refilling before returning to the field. This past year, we re-sent them with the same commitment we had made just five years before, but with a closer bond as we sought to repeat this process as their sending church.

The sending process is most tangibly seen when a special service of ordination or commissioning is held to recognize the external call. An individual has already been affirmed, so this service is a formal way to acknowledge they have gifts and are called to the work of ministry. The service may contain vows repeated by those being sent and by the congregation sending them.[35] The service should include a sermon that points to the biblical qualifications required, the work and ministry they are called to do, or the responsibility of the local church in affirming them. The content of the service can vary, offering instruction, encouragement, and challenge to both the individual and the congregation.

The most important part of the service is the laying on of hands by the pastors and church leaders. As they lay their hands on them, they pray for them and the ministry to which they are called — following the model of the church in Antioch (Acts

13:3). The act of laying on hands and praying is not a mystical transfer that somehow changes the individual; it simply marks in a visible way the conclusion of a process of testing, training, and affirmation by the pastors and members of the congregation. It also shows that the authority Christ has given to his church is being extended to this individual. Basil Manly Jr., a founding father of The Southern Baptist Theological Seminary, emphasized the responsibility of the local church in identifying those who qualify as ministers of the gospel and how the laying on of hands symbolizes that authority: "In regard to these qualifications, the churches are usually better judges than the individual himself, and must exercise their judgment with prudence and fidelity, under a solemn sense of their accountability, and 'lay not careless hands on heads that cannot teach and will not learn.'"[36]

Here is one way I have explained the laying on of hands to our congregation, during a service of commission:

> In a few moments, we will do what the church in Antioch did as recorded in Acts 13:3. We will lay hands on each of you and pray, sealing our affirmation of you to pursue these opportunities of ministry by God's grace.

While the laying on of hands is not a supernatural event in which the individuals prayed for are now somehow more prepared for the task than before, it is significant. As pastors and leaders lay their hands on the individual, they should pray for these things:

- fruitfulness in ministering the gospel
- faithfulness in proclaiming God's word
- protection from Satan for them and their families
- the development of a growing zeal and passion for the work to which they've been called
- Christ's presence in them by his Spirit
- purity and a hatred of sin

- an ability to be faithful in loving their wives as Christ loved the church
- faithfulness in shepherding God's sheep
- the continuing advance of God's kingdom

All of this is significant because God will answer these prayers. He will empower those who ask for his help. Just like the church in Antioch, we, by faith, believe that as we send them out, the Spirit also sends them out (Acts 13:3–4).

## Conclusion

Allow me to add a final plea for this priority to find its way into every shepherd's ministry. It takes a pastor to recognize a pastor. As you look for those who have the gift to serve in pastoral ministry, try to set aside for a moment a person's apparent immaturity and discern who may have a special gift from God to teach his word and care for his people. Even if you don't have a formal process for identifying and training, you can start by taking this individual to the hospital with you. Let them tag along on your visits to shut-ins. When you sense that it's time, let them lead a Sunday school class or a small group Bible study where you can observe them. Begin teaching your congregation about the church's responsibility to identify and train candidates for ministry and church leadership.

The process begins with pastors. If pastors do not accept this role and make this a priority, who will? If pastors do not look to identify and train these leaders, who will? If pastors do not create a culture in the church to embrace this biblical responsibility, who will? Although this task is largely ignored in a busy pastor's life, it must be taken on if the leaders of the next generation are to be equipped to lead as Christ calls and Scripture prescribes.

# Conclusion

Keep watch over yourselves and all the flock of which
the Holy Spirit has made you overseers.        **Acts 20:28**

Pastors are busy, and the demands of ministry are great. In this
book I've tried to summarize the essential aspects of a pastor's
ministry, as well as their significance, and I have offered practical
ways to begin engaging in them. This book is not intended to be
a comprehensive guide to every aspect of ministry. But I do hope
it has provided a keener vision so you can end up with a balanced
and biblical understanding of your pastoral ministry as a shepherd
serving under the Chief Shepherd.

There is a key factor that will determine your faithfulness in
carrying out these tasks. The truth is that you can be the most
gifted and beloved leader, but if you fail in this area, those gifts
will not help you. As a pastor, you need to have a dual focus, one
that is well summarized by Paul in his words of farewell to the
pastors in Ephesus:

> "Now I know that none of you among whom I
> have gone about preaching the kingdom will ever
> see me again. Therefore, I declare to you today that I
> am innocent of the blood of any of you. For I have not
> hesitated to proclaim to you the whole will of God.
> *Keep watch over yourselves and all the flock of which the
> Holy Spirit has made you overseers.* Be shepherds of the
> church of God, which he bought with his own blood.
> I know that after I leave, savage wolves will come in

among you and will not spare the flock. Even from your
own number men will arise and distort the truth in order
to draw away disciples after them. So be on your guard!
Remember that for three years I never stopped warning
each of you night and day with tears."

**Acts 20:25 – 31, italics added**

Earlier, we discussed the importance of the second part of the
charge Paul gives in Acts 20:28: "Keep watch over . . . *all the flock*"
(italics added). My final admonishment is the first part of the
charge: "Keep watch over *yourselves*" (italics added). Paul wrote
similar words to his young protégé, Timothy: "Watch your life
and doctrine closely. Persevere in them, because if you do, you
will save both yourself and your hearers" (1 Timothy 4:16). The
way Timothy saves himself and his hearers is to persevere in *life*
and *doctrine*.

Far too many pastors—even those who affirm and give priority to the responsibilities outlined in this book—spend much of
their time, energy, and devotion keeping watch over their flock.
Yet they do this to the detriment of their own souls. Pastors are
not invincible, though many act as though they are. The failure to
keep watch over your own life is not a minor matter; it is utterly
essential. Failure in this area will lead to burnout, discouragement, exhaustion, and great struggles with sin. Further neglect
can lead to decisions that wreck your ministry, your marriage, and
your life. Many pastors have been disqualified from the ministry
because they failed to watch over their own hearts; they failed to
preach to themselves and neglected their own relationship with
the Lord.

The most important area for a pastor to watch over is his relationship with God, his need to cultivate a deep, genuine, transparent, and heartfelt daily walk with Jesus. Pastors are first and
foremost individuals who have been transformed by the gospel of
Jesus. They need grace. They need forgiveness. They need peace
in their soul.

This investment of time is not something a pastor does just to have a better ministry, though it will likely make him a better man, husband, father, and pastor of his flock. But walking passionately with Jesus every day is something every pastor needs, and it is an amazing and precious gift from the heavenly Father.

You as a pastor have the deep honor and joy of walking with Jesus, receiving his immeasurable grace, battling your sin in the power God provides, and fervently pleading with the Father in prayer. Be honest with God about your own sin and brokenness, and read his word for the sole purpose of feeding your own soul, not simply to have a word to share with others. Believe the promises in God's word. They aren't just true for your people; they are God's word to you!

Consider several other practical actions that will prove to be good for your soul:

- *Keep watch over eating in a healthy manner, getting enough sleep, and engaging in regular exercise.* These are three of the most commonly neglected areas among pastors, and they can have a deeply negative impact on the disposition and energy of a pastor.
- *Keep watch over authentic friendships.* A pastor needs friends both inside and outside his church, relationships in which he can be honest, transparent, and bold in sharing the ways he struggles.
- *Keep watch over extended times of rest.* Take all of your vacation time—not some of it, *all of it.* I'm not joking. This will be a real benefit to you, your family, and even your church.
- *Keep watch over silence and solitude.* A helpful antidote to busyness is to stop, sit in a quiet place, be silent, and take some deep breaths to calm your spirit. Don't underestimate the daily benefits of this discipline.
- *Keep watch over the family.* A pastor's neglect of his family is not the result of busyness, but an indictment of his

heart. Watching over one's family is a discipline, and something we need to watch over closely if we hope to continue in this work (1 Timothy 3:4–5).

Pastors who take seriously Paul's exhortation to keep watch over themselves will in turn be more faithful and empowered to keep watch over the flock. Consider Charles Bridges's words from his classic work, *The Christian Ministry*:

> The most effectual hindrances, therefore, to our work are those which impede our personal communion with the Lord. When the great enemy thus successfully intercepts our spiritual supplies, the work of God in our hearts, and connected with it, the work of God in our hands, languishes from the want of its accustomed and needful support. We have great need to watch, lest public activity should be considered to atone for neglect of private intercourse with God; and thus our profession should become a snare to ourselves, and divested of all spiritual savor to our flock.[37]

Brothers, let us be pastors who do more than just faithfully care for the flock; let us also be heartfelt and passionate followers of the Chief Shepherd himself. Let us love him most and commune with him first. Let us look to him in all our failures, sin, and brokenness. When Christ appears for his redeemed flock in all his power, we will be filled with great joy, for we "will receive the crown of glory that will never fade away" (1 Peter 5:4). May that day come soon! Until it does, may we labor faithfully in the power that God provides, attending to all of the biblical responsibilities of a shepherd of God's flock.

# Acknowledgments

Brian would like to thank:

Zondervan for your partnership and ongoing investment in these practical resources for pastors.

H. B. Charles Jr. for your friendship and valuable contribution to this book.

Those who read through this manuscript and gave such valuable feedback, especially pastors. I am grateful for all who helped craft this book so it could assist those laboring in pastoral ministry.

All the wise older pastors who allowed me to sit at their feet and learn. This book is a compilation of your ongoing influence and investment in me.

Auburndale Baptist Church for the great honor of allowing me to be your pastor. This book would not exist without the gift of your fellowship and your willingness to share your life with me.

My wife and children for the many sacrifices you make so that I may pursue my ministry, the grace you give when I fail to care for you as I should, and the great joy you are as we walk through this unique life together.

The Chief Shepherd and my Redeemer, Jesus. Regardless of what happens in pastoral ministry, I always have you. That is enough.

# Notes

1. The New Testament uses the terms *pastor, elder, bishop,* and *overseer* interchangeably to refer to this one office of pastor/shepherd.

2. The three most common positions in interpreting the Sermon on the Mount are as follows: (1) Jesus is simply exposing the true intent of the law; (2) Jesus is radicalizing the meaning of the law; or (3) Jesus is creating an entirely new law. All three views affirm Jesus' fulfillment of the law of Moses and the truth that he was given full authority from the Father to define the purpose of the law.

3. I first heard this quote from my friend and mentor, Mark Dever. It is a paraphrase of a quote from a message by D. A. Carson: "One generation believes the gospel. The next generation assumes the gospel. The following generation denies the gospel."

4. Karen Willoughby, "Mohler's Utah Visit a 'Boost' to Pastors," *Baptist Press* online, www.bpnews.net/42331/mohlers-utah-visit-a -boost-to-pastors (accessed August 21, 2014).

5. Quoted in Ron Forseth, "Just What Is Pulpit Plagiarism?" *Church Leaders* online, www.churchleaders.com/pastors/pastor -articles/138301-just-what-is-pulpit-plagiarism.html (accessed August 22, 2014).

6. Quoted in Tim Brown, "The Preacher and Plagiarism," *Cross Connection Network* online, www.crossconnection.net/2011/10 /preacher-plagiarism/ (accessed August 22, 2014).

7. Joseph Belcher, ed., *The Complete Works of the Rev. Andrew Fuller with a Memoir of His Life by Andrew Gunton Fuller* (1845; repr., Harrisonburg, VA: Sprinkle, 1988), 3:201.

8. Iain H. Murray, *Archibald G. Brown: Spurgeon's Successor* (Edinburgh: Banner of Truth, 2011), 361.

9. A. W. Tozer, *Tragedy in the Church: The Missing Gifts* (Chicago: Moody, 2007), 22.

10. David Dickson, *The Elder and His Work* (1883; repr., Phillipsburg, NJ: P & R, 2004), 58.

11. Thomas Murphy, *Pastoral Theology: The Pastor in the Various Duties of His Office* (Philadelphia: Presbyterian Board of Publication, 1877), 242–43.

12. Ibid., 246–47.

13. Quoted in James M. Garretson, *An Able and Faithful Ministry: Samuel Miller and the Pastoral Office* (Grand Rapids: Reformation Heritage, 2014), 346.

14. Curtis Thomas, *Practical Wisdom for Pastors: Words of Encouragement and Counsel for a Lifetime of Ministry* (Wheaton, IL: Crossway, 2001), 104.

15. C. H. Spurgeon, Susannah Spurgeon, and W. J. Harrald, *C. H. Spurgeon's Autobiography* (1899; repr., Pasadena, TX: Pilgrim Publications, 1992), 1:371.

16. Ibid., 1:372.

17. Ibid., 1:371.

18. For detailed explanations of these five elements of a funeral, see Brian Croft and Phil Newton, *Conduct Gospel-Centered Funerals* (Grand Rapids: Zondervan, 2014), 42–48.

19. I first heard this advice from my mentor, Mark Dever. I don't know whether this is original with him.

20. John Flavel, Sermon 37 in "The Fountain of Life," in *The Works of John Flavel* (Carlisle, PA: Banner of Truth, 1997), 1:466.

21. Richard Baxter, *The Practical Works of the Rev. Richard Baxter* (London: Paternoster, 1830), 1:121.

22. Brian Croft and Austin Walker, *Care for Widows* (Wheaton, IL: Crossway, forthcoming, 2015).

23. Charles H. Spurgeon, *Autobiography, Volume 1: The Early Years, 1834–1859* (1898; repr., Edinburgh: Banner of Truth, 1962), 43–45.

24. Martin Bucer, *Concerning the True Care of Souls* (1538; repr., Edinburgh: Banner of Truth, 2009), 171.

25. Arnold Dallimore, *George Whitefield: The Life and Times of the Great Evangelist of the 18th Century Revival* (Carlisle, PA: Banner of Truth, 2001), 1:550.

26. Titus 1:6–9 and 1 Peter 5:1–4 are clear, complementary passages describing these biblical qualifications, though 1 Timothy 3:1–7 is our main focus in this chapter.

27. Richard Baxter, *The Reformed Pastor* (1656; repr., Edinburgh: Banner of Truth, 2001), 53.

28. C. H. Spurgeon, *Lectures to My Students* (1889; repr., Grand Rapids: Zondervan, 1954), 26.

29. Ibid., 26–27.

30. Ibid., 26.

31. John Angell James, *An Earnest Ministry* (1847; repr., Edinburgh: Banner of Truth, 1993), 222–23.

32. Roger Ellsworth, "Preach the Word," in *Dear Timothy: Letters on Pastoral Ministry* ed. Thomas K. Ascol (Cape Coral, FL: Founders Press, 2004), 272.

33. Michael A. G. Haykin, Roger D. Duke, and A. James Fuller, *Soldiers of Christ: Selections from the Writings of Basil Manly, Sr., and Basil Manly, Jr.* (Cape Coral, FL: Founders Press, 2009), 174.

34. Bucer, *Concerning the True Care of Souls*, 63.

35. For a helpful example, see Mark Dever and Paul Alexander, *The Deliberate Church: Building Your Ministry on the Gospel* (Wheaton, IL: Crossway, 2005), 158–59.

36. Haykin, Duke, and Fuller, *Soldiers of Christ*, 174.

37. Charles Bridges, *The Christian Ministry, with an Inquiry into the Causes of Its Inefficiency* (1830; repr., Edinburgh: Banner of Truth, 1967), 150.

# The Pastor's Family

Shepherding Your Family
through the Challenges of
Pastoral Ministry

*Brian Croft and Cara Croft*

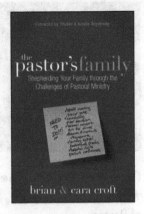

Featuring insights from the perspective of both a pastor and his wife—*The Pastor's Family* identifies the complicated burdens and expectations ministry brings to the life of a family. Brian and Cara Croft identify the unique challenges that pastors face as husbands and fathers. They also discuss the difficulties and joys of being a pastor's wife and offer practical advice on raising children in a ministry family. In addition to addressing the challenges of marriage and raising children, they also highlight the joys of serving together as a family and the unique opportunities pastors have to train their children and lead their families.

With discussion questions for use by couples and pastoral reading groups, this book is ideal for pastors and their spouses, pastoral ministry students and their wives, as well as elders, deacons, and others who wish to remain faithful to the care of their families while diligently fulfilling their calling in ministry. *The Pastor's Family* equips pastors with time-tested wisdom to address the tension of family and congregational dynamics while persevering in their calling.

*Available in stores and online!*

# Practical
## Shepherding

Brian Croft, series editor
www.practicalshepherding.com

## Prepare Them to Shepherd

Test, Train, Affirm, and Send the Next Generation
of Pastors

*Brian Croft*

In *Prepare Them to Shepherd*, pastor Brian Croft unpacks
the biblical model for preparing individuals for full-time ministry. This insightful book gives pastors and ministry leaders
practical help for testing, training, affirming, and sending those called into ministry.

## Visit the Sick

Ministering God's Grace in Times of Illness

*Brian Croft*

*Visit the Sick* gives pastors, church leaders, and caregivers
the biblical, theological, pastoral, and practical tools they need
to navigate through both the spiritual and physical care of the
sick and dying.

## Conduct Gospel-Centered Funerals

Applying the Gospel at the Unique Challenges
of Death

*Brian Croft and Phil Newton*

In *Conduct Gospel-Centered Funerals*, experienced pastors Brian Croft and Phil Newton offer readers a concise guide
to conducting funerals that glorify God and offer a timely message of hope.

## Gather God's People

Understand, Plan, and Lead Worship
in Your Local Church

*Brian Croft and Jason Adkins*

Gather God's People helps readers to understand how to apply biblical doctrine and spirituality to the practice of Christian worship.

---

## Comfort the Grieving

Ministering God's Grace in Times of Loss

*Paul Tautges*

In *Comfort the Grieving*, experienced pastor Paul Tautges offers readers a guide to comforting those dealing with death through the hope of the gospel.

---

## Pray for the Flock

Ministering God's Grace through Intercession
*Available summer 2015

*Brian Croft and Ryan Fullerton*

In *Pray for the Flock*, pastors Brian Croft and Ryan Fullerton provide biblical encouragement, practical advice, and helpful suggestions that will help busy pastors effectively pray for their people and care for their church through the ministry of intercession.

---

## Oversee God's People

Shepherding the Flock through Administration
and Delegation
*Available summer 2015

*Brian Croft and Bryce Butler*

In *Oversee God's People*, pastors Brian Croft and Bryce Butler unpack the Bible's teachings about administration and delegation in congregational leadership, offering the useful suggestions to improve the structures, process, and relationships among leaders in your church.

*Available in stores and online!*

Discipleship
**FAT**

Faithful

Available

Teachable